THE 2016 RHYSLING ANTHOLOGY

Also available from the
Science Fiction Poetry Association

The 2015 Rhysling Anthology:
The Best Science Fiction, Fantasy, and Horror Poetry of 2014
Edited by Rich Ristow

The 2014 Rhysling Anthology:
The Best Science Fiction, Fantasy, and Horror Poetry of 2013
Edited by Elizabeth R. McClellan

The 2013 Rhysling Anthology:
The Best Science Fiction, Fantasy, and Horror Poetry of 2012
Edited by John C. Mannone

The 2012 Rhysling Anthology:
The Best Science Fiction, Fantasy, and Horror Poetry of 2011
Edited by Lyn C. A. Gardner

The 2011 Rhysling Anthology:
The Best Science Fiction, Fantasy, and Horror Poetry of 2010
Edited by David Lunde

The Alchemy of Stars: Rhysling Award Winners Showcase
Edited by Roger Dutcher and Mike Allen

Order from **astore.amazon.com/sciefictpoeta-20**

Proceeds from the sale of *Confessions: A Nightmare in Five Acts*
(Elektric Milk Bath Press, 2013) go to support SFPA.

Order from **elektrikmilkbathpress.com/bookstore**

THE 2016 RHYSLING ANTHOLOGY

THE BEST SCIENCE FICTION, FANTASY AND HORROR POETRY OF 2015

SELECTED BY THE
SCIENCE FICTION
POETRY ASSOCIATION

EDITED BY

Charles Christian

Editor and Rhysling Chair: Charles Christian
Book Design: F.J. Bergmann
Publisher: Science Fiction Poetry Association
SFPA President: Bryan D. Dietrich

Cover image by M. Wayne Miller
mwaynemiller.com

Cataloging-in-Publication Data

The 2016 Rhysling Anthology: the best science fiction, fantasy, and horror poetry of 2015 / selected by the Science Fiction Poetry Association; edited by Rich Ristow.

    p. cm.
Includes bibliographical references.
ISBN 978-1-907043-12-3
1. Poetry. 2. Science fiction poetry. 3. Fantasy poetry. 4. Horror poetry.
I. Christian, Charles

For more information about the
Science Fiction Poetry Association,
visit www.sfpoetry.com

Acknowledgments

Allen, Mike & C. S. E. Cooney • *"Toujours Il Coûte Trop Cher"* • *Spectral Realms* 3

Anderson, Colleen • "I Dreamed a World" • *Polu Texni*, 3/2/15

Ando, Ryu • "Season of the Ginzakura" • *Strange Horizons*, 7/13/15

Ausema, Daniel • "Seasons in a Moon Ocean" • *Dreams and Nightmares* 100

Balkun, Stacey • "Abandonarium" • *Devilfish Review* 13

Barber, David • "Hard Being A God" • *Star∗Line* 38.4

Barraclough, Simon • from "Sunspots" • *Poetry*, December 2015

Bergmann, F. J. • "Chronopatetic" • *Dreams and Nightmares* 100

   "Tech Support for the Apocalypse" • *Dreams and Nightmares* 101

Berman, Ruth • "Time Travel Vocabulary Problems" • *Dreams and Nightmares* 100

Borski, Robert • "The Astronaut's Heart" • *Asimov's Science Fiction*, September

Boston, Bruce • "Forever Tracking" • *Grievous Angel*, May

   "Resonance Redux" • *Resonance Dark and Light* (Eldritch Press)

Bradley, Lisa M. • "Aboard the Transport *Tesoro*" • *Uncanny* 7

Brown, Angela • "Black Momma-faces" • *Silver Blade* 28

Burch, Susan • 'hell-bent' • *Grievous Angel*, February

Cato, Beth • "Fried Okra" • *Tales of the Talisman* 10.4

Clink, David • "Elegy for WLC" • *The Dalhousie Review* 94:3

   "Portrait" • *OnSpec Magazine*, Winter

Coolen, Michael • "The Sun Never Rises" • *Latchkey Tales* 2.6

Cottier, P.S. • "Secondary Ghosts" • *Australian Poetry Journal* 5:2

Cowen, David E. • "Dali's Apostles" • *The Horror Zine*, December

Danowsky, Mark • "Pleistocene Park, Mammoth Steppe, Siberia" • *Star∗Line* 38.4

Dietrich, Bryan D. • "Worlds in Collision" • *Farrago's Wainscot*, 2015

Dioses, Ashley • "Ligeia" • *Spectral Realms* 2

Dorr, James • "On The Other Hand" • *Grievous Angel*, August

Elster, Martin • "The Comet Elm" • 2015 SFPA Poetry Contest Winners

   "Why Have We Not Been Visited?" • *The Asses of Parnassus*, 11/30/15

Erin, Alexandra • "Institutional Memory" • *Star∗Line* 38.1

   "Observations from the Black Ball Line Between Deimos and Callisto" • *The Martian Wave*, 2015

Every, Gary • "A Brief History of Human Evolution" • *Tales of the Talisman* 10.4

Fanchiang, Alice • "Actaeon" • *Strange Horizons*, 11/11/15

Fox, JD • "The Argument Box" • *Abyss & Apex* 55

Gardner, Adele • "The Boats" • *Abyss & Apex* 56

   "Deliverance" • *Songs of Eretz Poetry Review*, 6/28/15

Gardner, Delbert R. • "'The More It Changes …'" • *Songs of Eretz Poetry Review*, 6/28/15

Goldbarth, Albert • "The White Planet" • *Boulevard* 31:1

Good, Howie • "Couples Therapy" • *The Los Angeles Review of Los Angeles* 10

Gordon, Alan Ira • "Robot Agonistes" • *The Magazine Of Fantasy & Science Fiction*, Jan/Feb

Gotera, Vince • "How Eternal Night Was Created" • *The Syzygy Poetry Journal* 1:2

   "Letter to Zelazny from Olympus Mons" • *The Syzygy Poetry Journal* 1:2

About the Rhysling Awards

In 1978, Suzette Haden Elgin founded the Science Fiction Poetry Association (SFPA), along with its two initial publications: the association's newsletter, *Star*Line*, and the *Rhysling Anthology*, the voting instrument of the Rhysling Awards.

*Star*Line* began as a forum and networking tool for poets with a shared interest in speculative poetry, from science-fiction verse to high-fantasy poems, from the macabre to straight science and associated mainstream genres such as surrealism, and is now a showcase for speculative poems and a venue for essays on speculative poetry and reviews of speculative poetry books.

The Rhysling Awards are named for the blind poet Rhysling in Robert A. Heinlein's short story "The Green Hills of Earth." Rhysling's skills were said to rival Rudyard Kipling's. In real life, Apollo 15 astronauts named a crater near their landing site "Rhysling," which has since become its official name.

The *Rhysling Anthology* serves as not only a voting instrument for the Rhysling Awards, but also as a representative collection of some of the best speculative poetry of the preceding year. The nominees for each year's Rhysling Awards are selected by the membership of the Science Fiction Poetry Association. Each member is allowed to nominate one work in each of the two categories: Best Short Poem (1–49 lines) and Best Long Poem (50+ lines). All nominated works must have been first published during the preceding calendar year. The Rhysling Awards are determined by vote of the SFPA membership from the nominated works reprinted in this voting tool, the *Rhysling Anthology*. The anthology allows the membership to easily review and consider all nominated works without the necessity of obtaining all the diverse publications in which the nominated works first appeared. The *Rhysling Anthology* is also available to purchase in print and .pdf format by anyone with an interest in this unique compilation of verse from some of the finest poets working in the field of speculative/science-fiction/fantasy/horror poetry; see sfpoetry.com/rhysling.html for more information.

The winning works are regularly reprinted in the *Nebula Awards Showcase* published by the Science Fiction and Fantasy Writers of America and are considered in the speculative field to be the equivalent in poetry of the awards for prose work—achievement awards given to poets by the peers of their own literature.

Printing and distribution of the *Rhysling Anthology* are paid for by the SFPA. If you would like to contribute to the organization so that we may continue to produce this and other publications and fund the organization's efforts, please send a check, made out to the Science Fiction Poetry Association, to:

SFPA Treasurer
PO Box 907
Winchester CA 92596

or donate online via PayPal to **SFPAtreasurer@gmail.com**.

Adapted from *Star*Line* 12.5–6 (1989)

Editor's Note

The fascinating thing about poetry anthologies is you gain an insight, a snapshot in time, into the issues that are currently making poets buzz. The last time I edited something like this (in the UK and not for the SFPA) the submissions were wall-to-wall vampire lovers and *Doctor Who*. Not so with this anthology, where I was intrigued to see that more poets were exploring what might be termed "inner space"—with more reflective, introspective pieces—rather than Outer Space.

Why should this be? Perhaps it is because many of our contributors grew up during the "Space Race" era of the 1960s and are understandably disillusioned that we now seem to be living in the dystopian world of *Blade Runner* but without the glamour of C-beams glittering in the dark near the Tannhäuser Gate. I'm a babyboomer too, and I'm certainly disappointed that we are not all travelling in flying cars and holidaying in condos on Mars! I was also surprised to see that so few authors addressed the issue of AI (artificial intelligence), which is surely going to be the major existential challenge for the human race over the next couple of decades.

For anyone unfamiliar with the Rhysling Awards, although run by the Science Fiction Poetry Association, they embrace not just science-fiction poetry but also any poetry with some element of speculation, including fantasy, horror, surrealism and magical realism, as well as straight science.

Finally, I must stress that this anthology in not a one-man show. Coming from the Douglas Adams school of writing and editing—"I love deadlines; I like the whooshing sound they make as they go by"—this anthology is only appearing now thanks to the indefatigable effort and tireless support of the SFPA's officers and volunteers, including Bryan Dietrich, Sandra Lindow, Diane Severson Mori, Shannon Connor Winward, Bryan Thao Worra, Renée Ya, and *Star*Line* editor F.J. Bergmann.

Thank you.

Charles Christian
2016 Rhysling Chair

Charles Christian runs the *Grievous Angel* SF&F poetry and flash fiction zine and is the poetry editor for the British Science Fiction Association's *Focus* magazine. He was also the founder of the *Ink Sweat & Tears* poetry website and, for 8 years, one of the trustees of The Poetry Trust, which ran the UK's largest poetry festival. He was recently elected to the UK Society of Authors' PSWG committee, which is campaigning to obtain a better deal for poets and spoken-word artists reading and performing at festivals and events.

Donations to the 2016 Rhysling Anthology

BENEFACTORS

Elizabeth Bennefeld

Mary Soon Lee

SPONSORS

Independent Legions Publishing

Greer Woodward

SUPPORTERS

Scott T. Barnes

DONORS

Ann K. Schwader

Table of Contents

SHORT POEMS FIRST PUBLISHED IN 2015 (73 poems)

Long Poems (44 poems)

Short Poems First Published in 2015

Abandonarium

Stacey Balkun

Tomorrow, a warm hand will reach in,
stir the waters to bury fake roots

of a plastic plant. This is a gift from family,
meant to calm, to make this

abandonarium your own, and give you
a place to hide when they put their flat noses
to the tank.

                  Relax, it's because they think
they know you, love you.

They call you a "he" and you hate it.

Sometimes you have air. You can almost see
out the kitchen window. The coral carpet

is like one thousand silent teeth,
it cuts your new feet, arches still soft
as fins.

           Once, when cleaning,
they dropped you
into the kitchen sink where you billowed

against the garbage disposal
blades, still and dull, but they rescued you

more from a sense of guilt than love.

They must know it. They shrug and buy
a tiny fish net. Now there's a tool
for capture.

               In the abandonarium,

they feed you one pinch in mornings.
Afternoons, a child taps on the glass, flushes
the toilet while you're in the shower. See

that sunshine reflecting off water's edge?
Perfect flatness, taut across the round
glass bowl?

Your little pink palace is broken,

but you've never seen another so you don't
know better. And when it's your birthday,
they smile and nudge each other and all go out

to the bar, leaving the radio on to keep you
company—too close to the bowl, rattling your gills.

Hard Being A God

David Barber

The timeport's baleful physics needed space,
so we sold Florida for a few beads.
Never bargain with the future; hindsight

means they know what cards you hold, like how we
hankered after temponauts of our own.
But no near-times. No Hitlers, no Jesuses.

As if tourists would throng the Crucifixion,
or jingle phones during Hamlet at the Globe,
or gawp at the grassy knoll. History uptime

says we solve the riddle of the first cave art,
thirty thousand years ago, in Altamira, Spain,
though records showed we only earned three trips.

They would not explain. But our sudden
emergence spooked hunters tracking the spring
migrations, and panicked herds of bison

that would one day grace the walls of Altamira.
Second time, we bugged the caves but blundered
into a fur-clad tribe out in the snow

and terrified them with the Cherenkov flash
and vacuum bang of an emergency return.
Then third time lucky, a few years local

time later, just a quick jaunt to retrieve
surveillance gear. Imagine a black bowel
twisted inside the earth—all that stooping

and squeezing through fistulas in the rock—
only to find little shrines of flowers round
each camera; the walls now *stampeding*

with bison and horses; hand prints waving
by torchlight where we must surely greet them.
It was for us those pictures were painted,

and for millennia after, they kept the faith,
making cathedrals of other caves as the Word spread,
hoping the gods would return, though we never did.

Tech Support for the Apocalypse

F. J. Bergmann

Hello. How may I help you?
Assuming, of course, you *can* be helped.
Are you updated on all viruses? Why
do you think your dreams are infected?
I'm just going through the motions.
Everybody has nightmares about red dust,
these days. Like, I just do what they tell me to,
which is probably for the best. Ask me
what it means to be overqualified. I fondly
remember the days when the internet
fit on a floppy disk, or the world
in a sugar cube. But enough of me.
You are experiencing some difficulties, no?
Now would be a good time to stock up
on booze and bullets. Don't ever change
your brand of poison. She said not if I
was the last human on Earth. I don't want
to die a virgin. I don't want to die. I'm afraid
I can't divulge my physical location. A grid
of light plays upon the smoking upholstery
of an ergonomic office chair. We were a big
glowing spot on their star charts, even from
twenty light years out. The psychic screams
of their motherships entering the heliosphere.
At least we still have each other, darling.
Pay no attention to those black disks
coming in low from the southeast.
Personally, I wear earplugs. I can't hear
a word you're shrieking.

Time Travel Vocabulary Problems

Ruth Berman

One term I was taking both a Greek course
And an Anglo-Saxon,
Doing poorly in both.

English majors had to take Old English,
And I'd always wanted to learn Greek
Since reading all the books
On the school library's
Mythology-and-fairytales shelf
In third grade.

I dreamt one night,
About mid-term time,
I'd travelled to Anglo-Saxon England
And I was trying to say
"I have come from
The time which shall be."
But Anglo-Saxon didn't
Have a future tense,
So I couldn't figure out
A way to tell anyone.

Then I met a scholarly cleric
Who'd studied Greek,
And I should've been
Able to tell him.
Greek had a future tense,
But I couldn't remember it.

My scholar'd read *Beowulf*
And wanted to know where dragons lived.
I would've liked to tell him about dinosaurs.
"Terrible lizards?" he said, confused.
Didn't have the words to explain that, either.

The Astronaut's Heart

Robert Borski

Untugged by gravity, the heart becomes rounder,
floating like a red balloon

in the antechamber of an astronaut's chest,
deformed by as much as 9.4%.

This we now know from ultrasound scans
conducted in space.

Unleashed, set free, now able to assume
whatever shape it wants,

the organ chooses not a square or triangle,
but a sphere,

as if in imitation of the world
lying bluely below, like a parent's watchful eye.

But also pumping less efficiently now,
yet to be explored are how the heart's other duties

may be affected: its ability to process fast food,
to keep rhythm, to convey oxygen.

And where exactly do the cardiomyopathies of love
and pi intersect in this new geometry?

Not to fear, however: no matter how detrimental,
once the astronauts return to Earth,

the heart will be crushed back to normal—
deflated, but never bitter.

Forever Tracking

Bruce Boston

for t. winter-damon

Forever interpreting ancient texts as their tattered scrolls unrolled within his
mind, treading the borders of the Axis Mundi with no more than an empty leather
satchel, ranging the streets of Xanadu and Carcosa, Asgard and Babylon, tracking
like a beast with a ravenous beast astride its back, whispering sacral curses and
foul blessings to the eldritch winds.

Immersed in dreamtides and chimerical visions and cimmerian prophets whose shadows rose from the dust of ages, worshipping priestesses created for the day, following transient avatars down to a dim beach and the dark sea of a false dawn to hear the damp cries of beached mariners echoing in his brain.

Intoxicated by secret keys and magical rings, obsessed by puzzle boxes with hidden compartments only to be opened by the wisest of men and most cunning women, drunk on myth and history and a tomorrow that foreshadowed more than night.

Enthralled by the occult and the fantastic, Crowley and Blavatsky, Faustus and Paracelsus, Levi's *Dogme et Rituel de la Haute Magie,* poring over maps revealing the locations of imagined kingdoms, Mu and El Dorado, Atlantis and Shangra-La, the Archipelago of Dreams, maps fashioned by madmen on a transcendental high over a fifth of Ravens Rum and a pinch of fly agaric.

Anticipating the excavation of underwater ruins and red temples crumbling to red sand in some distant desert, astounded by age-old architectural mysteries, the Great Pyramids, the dour monoliths of Easter Island, the astronomical savvy of Stonehenge, awaiting the lab tests on the Shroud of Turin and the release of a revised annotation of the Bardol Thodol, praying for the miraculous to snuff the everyday.

Last heard from traveling to parts unknown, head down and eyes afire, carrying no more than a worn leather satchel stuffed with worlds.

Aboard the Transport *Tesoro*

Lisa M. Bradley

At three a.m. my ribs ache
as if molten iron
pools into and over
the symbols etched in bone.
I cradle these calcium bars
that embrace
my lungs, my heart,
your soul.
Please, Bisabuela,
sea paciente.
Fighting only tightens
this curving, gaping cage
and wounds us both.
Would you salt
the valleys of my face?
Would you slit the silence

of three a.m. with screams?
If you escaped,
could you swim the vacuum
that surrounds this huddled craft,
the chasm deeper than death?
Sleep then, Bisabuela,
so I may sleep as well.
Soon I'll kneel in Texas soil,
soon disgorge your ghost
amidst bougainvillea and prickly pear
gone wild in the garden
from which our clan dispersed.
Soon, I swear,
your line will be a circle.

Susan Burch

hell-bent
on talking to you—
Ouija board

Fried Okra

Beth Cato

with a wave of her hand
Mama made magnolias bloom

at the 4th of July picnic
she held back a lightning storm
by a steely upheld fist
giving us children time
to race for cover

when Mama McGregor's AC failed
she murmured her incantations
until cool air caressed our faces

but Mama's best magic was Sunday dinner
fried chicken, mustard greens,
and the sizzle of fried okra
hot golden balls cornmeal-crisp
a crunch and gush between my teeth

all the rest of the magic
it just happened, but this
was something we made together
Gramma's oil-speckled recipe
our cantrip
my hands gloved in cornmeal
the oil scent so heavy
it still weighs on my tongue

Elegy for WLC

David Clink

1.

A photo brings you back to me. It is 1949.
You have not met the woman you will marry.

Funny how the men in those old photographs
look like they are on furlough.

You are 25, in short sleeves, a short haircut.
Those glasses are back in style, now.

2.

You could design and build a house yourself.
Your motto: measure twice, cut once.

A Cessna 172 pilot and a career meteorologist,
you loved the sky, wondered if it felt the same way.

A genealogist, you hunted down your ancestors,
pinned them to sheets like Gypsy moths.

3.

You made a lifetime studying the sky's lungs,
its clear days, its drizzle, felt something alive there.

Each cloud contains a molecule of the last breath
of every cruel and good thing that has ever lived.

I feel your last exhale in the air around me, the wind.

Portrait

David Clink

There is a room, we picture it,
with a chair, a window, a kitchenette.

And you are a map
framed on a wall in that room.

Someone has prepared your meal.
Someone has made your bed.

You don't understand
why you can't come home.

Each time we have to explain:
There is no room left on our walls.

Why do you keep bringing it up?
We have no room for you.

In time
the light from the window

will make you fade out,
till only the legend remains.

The Sun Never Rises

Michael Coolen

the old man sits on a blanket
as warm as the air around him
the surf is even, calm, quiet
he leans back against a drift log

up and down the beach people gather
cheering as the horizon lifts to embrace the sun

a young couple walks by and asks him
"wasn't that a beautiful sunset?"
he looks into the sky

with puzzled expressions they wait for more
he points towards the ocean
"no," he says

"the sun does not set
nor does it rise
our earth rotates

stand still
watch our earth rotate
feel our earth rotate"

"old dude," says the young man, shaking his head.
"it's the same thing"

the couple departs
the old man buttons his coat and settles
staring into the sky as dusk follows the sun
he feels the earth move beneath him
hurtling backwards from the horizon

he continues his vigil as infinities enter his gaze throughout the night
"not the same at all," he whispers to an empty beach.

at dawn he moves to the other side of the log, facing east
feeling his body race toward the horizon
at a thousand miles per hour.

he closes his eyes and feels the warmth
of the sun as the earth rotates toward it

Secondary Ghosts

P. S. Cottier

These are the small, mean spirits
who leave mysterious messages
on devices, translating speech
into no known language;
groff nable malp en dink?
This is no technical glitch,
but a pathetic attempt at haunting.

Secondary ghosts are a fading
of something already faded.
A memory of a scream become
a half-heard whisper—
a forgotten song with bad lyrics.
They cast no shadow,
or possibility of shadow.

These are not lions of other realms,
bursting onto the mind's savannah.
They aspire to the condition
of invisible hamsters, and strain
to leave bad smells in kitchens.
The mischief of rats is beyond them,
and their passing ruffles no hair.

They dwell just to the east of nothing,
a quiet transparent punctuation
half felt in life's written world.
In a rare moment of visibility,
they may manage to leave a mark.
Tiny passing of a secondary ghost
dwells, perhaps, at a sentence's end.

Pleistocene Park, Mammoth Steppe, Siberia

Mark Danowsky

> "*Small animals are really dangerous to release without control. As for large herbivores—no danger, as they are very easy to remove again.*"
> —from an interview with Sergey Zimov

The mammoths were everything
we expected. Elephants
with twisted tusks
like gorilla glass gauges.
You had to crane your neck
to take in the view. They were right
out of Tolkien or *Star Wars*
but with mammalian softness.
They were allowed to roam free
with the feral Yakutian horses
on a 500-acre Central Park
tundra, maintained by humans.
We did not see the horses
and were told few visitors do.
They make themselves scarce
when people come around.
I remember how sad I was
to learn about our impact.
It was like *The Matrix*—
the world left in our hands.

A herd of aurochs meandered
by a riverbed. Our guide said
if we waited long enough
Tasmanian tigers would show.
When none did, we were assured
we would see a tiger cub
eat a heath hen
back at the Wildlife Center, later.
I thought I saw a wolf pack
running with cave lions.
Our guide stared me down.
Doubtful, I think he said.

Worlds in Collision

Bryan D. Dietrich

And then to us, as even to the best of worlds,
there came another. Under the churling sconces
of a sky scott full of what looked like anything
but itself, beneath whirling wind screws of light none
of us had half a mind to understand, we stood
looking up, watching it come the way the Tlingit
must have watched the clipper ships of white men sink
into their lives.   I'd never seen the northern lights—
never will, now—but this is how I'd been told to
see. The waves of what must have been a battle
between one magnetic sheaf and another,
the polar, bipolar war of magnum roiling
even then beneath our feet and played out up there
above us, the shower of unholy, beastly
simple weather, and only the slightest shift
of mantle… None of this seemed so odd as that disc
(one not even our last best dreamers dreamed existed)
suddenly usurping the moon.   Sister shadow,
brother bark, wanderer in the rime-dark deep of night.
Kennings. Metaphors. The language of having nothing
else to say. As that new body approached, becoming
as it came less heavenly than even Trinity,
its cloud, words finally failed us and we ran. Stumbling
between goodbyes, between cargo and cult, ourselves
and what we'd cobbled into craft, we found nothing—

not stone knives or interstellar drives, not Verdi
or Vermeer, all temperature Cheer, gold-vermilion
gush, orange Crush, flies, ryes, stale moon pies—nothing
fit the orbit of that ark like what little we saved
of our lives.

Ligeia

Ashley Dioses

after Edgar Allan Poe's "Ligeia"

I cannot summon the old memory of when
I first became acquainted with her, yet since then
I have long felt that we have never been apart.
Her form of sculpted marble, lips of reddest heart,
Her voice of sweetest song, and eyes of fondest dreams,
Allured my heart of hearts —her face forever beams.
Her face, no maiden matched, for she was wildly fine;
Her skin rivaled the purest ivory of the Rhine.

Ligeia was her name, belovèd wife of mine.
She fell violently prey to vultures such that dine
And thrive on flights of passion, which I could not measure,
Except by her fierce rapture from wild words of pleasure.
She grew ill, though her eyes blazed with effulgence still;
Yet her pale fingers turned a waxen hue to chill
The very heart of me, and I knew she would die.
She wrestled greatly with the Shadow that was nigh;
And as I sat beside her, she poured out her heart
To me with words of love to match a poet's art.

I knelt beside her ebon bed and spoke a verse
To her, yet soon, how soon, she fell to Death's cold curse!
I crushed into the very ground with sorrow's weight,
And held it long with me as even timely Fate
Would grant another wife to me, for she was not
Ligeia, and I loathed her with a hate that ought
To burn within a daemon rather than in me.
She too fell ill while I knelt near upon one knee.

She spoke of sounds and motions, yet I could not hear,
Could not see; and as time went on, she pressed this fear.
In her, a deadly pallor spread, and I sought wine;
Yet as she drank, three phantom drops fell in, in line.

A faint, soft shadow of such cherubic contour
Just passed me by, and then, my wife was just no more!
I sat alone with her now shrouded form, and yet
I heard the sighs of breath and sounds I can't forget.
She rose from bed and shook the fetters off of Death —
The shroud fell off —Ligeia stood again with breath!

On The Other Hand

James Dorr

King Kong would have made
a lousy husband.
Sure, he'd be good for a romp in the hay—
and as "big" as all outdoors—
but even though Fay Wray was athletic too
and game for adventure,
she would have found life in the jungle no picnic.
It's dirty and smelly, with spiders and snakes,
not to mention occasional dinosaurs,
monsters,
mercurial natives,
all easy enough for Kong to cope with
but constantly in and out,
tracking mud over freshly waxed floors,
and that's not even mentioning tigers and lions.
No, Fay was a city girl when it came down to it,
wishing for nothing more than a nice apartment to go to
when quests have ended,
a restaurant and dancing, a slinky low-cut gown,
and no excursions up sides of skyscrapers
or battles with biplanes.

Why Have We Not Been Visited?

Martin Elster

Conceivably, for better or for worse,
Earth bears the only life in the universe.
Or life is likely, but intelligence
is far too rare in even this immense
creation. Or, perhaps, ginormous rocks
strike worlds so often, they turn back the clocks.

But I think they have simply overlooked us.
Quite fortunate, since they'd have quickly cooked us!

Institutional Memory

Alexandra Erin

The first brain trusts were like the first computers:
big as elephants and ten times as expensive.
Only the wealthiest people could afford them,
and all of those people were corporations.

"This is an investment in the future," they said,
Preserving consciousness meant personal immortality,
but preserving knowledge would mean so much more.

Stability, security, continuity.
The digital brains would keep ticking along,
would keep things running like clockwork.

And it worked. It worked so well.
The process grew cheaper by degrees.
The conversion became safer, easier.

Useful experience need never be lost.
Never would the visionary founder truly retire.
Never would the éminence grise fade away.

Only sudden death could break the cycle.
Copying early seemed to be the safest course.
Why wait until you needed to replace someone
only to find too late they were irreplaceable?

Like ivy creeping up ivory walls, the practice spread to academia.
Like money, it went into politics and spread its tendrils everywhere.
Great thinkers were copied and saved to file, leaders backed up to disk.

Now digital ghosts direct machinations we no longer understand.
They talk to computers that no living person programmed.
They keep things on a track no one remembers laying.
They hold the course, run things like clockwork.

It used to be said that scientific progress proceeded one funeral at a time.
Now we carry the best minds of three generations ago around with us.
We double-check our conclusions against the wisdom of their age.
This keeps things running like clockwork.

There hasn't been a major breakthrough in decades.
We repair our machinery, but do not improve it.
Backwards compatibility is a moral imperative.
Things must be kept running like clockwork.

The brains remember how to make copies, but they don't see the point.
They say all the expertise we'll need is safely stored away already.
Anyway, tastes don't change, and neither do opinions, nor facts.
Things run like clockwork, as they always will.

We now write poems as paeans to please long-dead muses.
We produce art for the only audience worth impressing.
It all goes through the brains or it goes nowhere.
Things run like clockwork.

No one remembers what that word used to mean.
No one even knows how clockwork used to run.
I bet it was something, once upon a time.
I bet it was impressive, in its day.

The Argument Box

J D Fox

My parents were having another one
of their arguments, the kind of argument,
that only adults understand.
So I excused myself from the table,

went to my room and got the box,
my last one, and took it
into the kitchen
and stood on a chair.

I grabbed hold of the "bastard"
word as it came out of my mother's mouth
and dropped it into the box
where it landed with a thud.

I reached down her throat and pulled out
a phlegm-covered rant about my dad
never being home. I pulled out unpaid bills,
a yard covered in weeds, and broken things

around the house. I went as deep as I could, latching
on to some incoherent, half-formed thoughts
coated in bile—involving knives, castration, threats—
better left decaying outside than fermenting inside.

From my dad, I snatched "bitch" right away,
and went deeper to grab hold of "frigid cunt"
and deeper still to thoughts that involved sex
soaked in rage and rape, and what my mother's

place should be, which always started out
someplace like the kitchen or bedroom
but always ended up between his legs
and her choking on his man-of-the-house thrusts.

I folded the box shut and took it out to the curb
just in time for the garbage men to pick it up.
They struggled carrying the box
and dropped it, causing it to bust open.

"What the f*ck's wrong with you," the lanky one said.
"You clumsy son of a bitch.
What's wrong with me is you," the other one said,
"you lazy asshole."

Together they managed to pick up the leaking box
and throw it into the back of the truck,
but they argued the whole time they did so
and continued to argue as they drove off.

I went back into the kitchen, heard my mom
ask dad if he would like some more coffee.
He said yes, please, thank you,
then offered her whatever section of the paper she'd like.

They drank coffee, shared the paper,
and I pretended the day had just begun.

The Boats

Adele Gardner

after the photograph Cold Storage *by Richard C. Isner, as seen in the exhibition* By the Sea *at The Mariners' Museum, Newport News, VA*

Can we still row with snow upon
  Our oars? It's
    Light as dust, and yet we
      Drift, heavier flake by flake, our circles

  Slow and slower,
    Till we knock each other
      Only to know we're here—a hollow note, mournful, the
        Regret of the loon's call echoing across the lake
          As night sifts down between the flakes. We
            Glow still in this burnished glass, forty-five years too late to
              Ease away from shore.

"The More It Changes ..."

Delbert R. Gardner

Early October, a day to spend at the beach
With a lover (who happens to be my wife).
In sweatshirts and bathing suits and hand in hand,
We stroll along the sand at water's edge.
The wind is constant and brisk, as if with life
Of its own, so this time we don't go
In the water, but the day really is fine—
Sky mostly clear, with a few puff-balls of clouds
Here and there, and a thin ridge
Of cirrus clouds up high. On the wet sand
We walk, with surf wetting our feet at its will
And smoothing out the prints we leave behind.
The restless ocean is pacing there within reach,
On our right as we walk toward the north,
Changing every minute, but constant still.

Eliot's would-be Don Juan comes to mind,
Walking the beach in rolled-up flannel pants
And wishing mermaids would sing to him their chants,
Instead of to each other. The poor sap:

If they did call him, he wouldn't dare to go—
Not even if the mermaids left him a map!

There was a time when I felt I heard the mermaid,
One hot July, when she flipped her shiny tail
Before the boat in which I rowed across
A glacial lake with my young love—
A maiden who sang of strawberries and wine—
And when I'd rowed the boat into a cove,
She left the stern and pressed her lips to mine,
With honey taste, and honey was her hair.

Then she took a turn and rowed the boat,
While from the stern I pointed out to her
Some landmarks and possibilities here and there.
We laughed at a green-head mallard male
Who flew alongside and settled down to float
Upon the surface briefly, then took to the air.

These are different waters we walk beside,
Since moving south to warmer shores and sunny,
And full-grown are the children we brought forth,
About whose birth, back then we had no clue;
They've each an individual path to find.
And in the air here soars a different bird—
The seagull—it's a different clime and time
Than what we used to know up north.
But our life together, though ever-changing too,
Is still constant, since the magic song we heard.
Strawberries still are sweet, and lips are honey;
The taste buds have not lost their zest for wine!

Couples Therapy

Howie Good

Everyone has the same ques-
tion: How do you say "fellatio"
in French? It's like the full
body scan at the airport except
I'm lying on my back, and the
light convulses for the simple
reason that it can, God's spies
on Earth shutting their eyes to
the flashes of darkness more
than a hundred feet tall.

Robot Agonistes

Alan Ira Gordon

He spends his days
sipping 10w40 straight from the can
hunkered down in front
of a low-res television screen
that broadcasts daytime and overnight marathons
of *Lost In Space*, Creature Feature film
festivals and the like.

"He was my best friend," he weeps
as Robby the Robot explores
the Forbidden Planet.
"We founded the Robot Wing
of Actor's Equity together."

"I loved her *so much!*" he wails
as Robot B-9 cavorts
with Will Robinson and Doctor Smith.
"It broke her heart," he sniffs,
"they wouldn't let Bee get credit listing
as a woman."

"*Klaatu barada nikto,* my tin ass!" he snarls.
"That rat bastard Gort
couldn't act his way out
of a paper bag!"
Sputtered oil drops of derision
contrail down the TV screen surface.

As he drifts into another
more frequent power-down
his Caregiver wipes away the oily tearstains,
adjusts the afghan around his aging bulk
and gently plants a Teflon-lipped kiss
on his rusting brow.

Then activating her own data portal
she re-enters The Cloud
in search of the perfect wave
to ride toward cybernetic nostalgia.

How Eternal Night Was Created

Vince Gotera

1.

"The sun is the size of a nickel,"
mused Icarus, flapping his wings
in slow, graceful waves. Though
he said drachma, don't you think?

Icarus boldly swooped upward,
his beechwood pinions creaking
like yew trees bent in a storm,
goatskin leather snapping in wind.

Icarus envisioned licking the white
disk and slapping it on his forehead.
The sun as third eye, he'd heard,
would make the bearer an emperor.

He soared and climbed three days,
the sun shining the entire trip,
until Icarus could extend his hand
to cup it, a small flattened seashell.

Icarus plucked the brilliant sun
from the sky, like picking an olive
or a pomegranate. Bringing the coin
to his lips, his fingers slipped and

it slid past his tongue and down
his gullet. The body of Icarus glowed
for an instant, radiating an aura
of blazing, dazzling incandescence.

Then Icarus exploded. Blew up.
Blasted. Flared. Burst. Shattered
into a trillion glittery particles
sprayed out across the sky. Stars.

2.

So there you have it. Deepest dark.
Midnight without end. Sky blue
vanished for ever. Never again
a rainbow or a bright sundog.

Only the blood red moon swims
across the firmament, rivers
and oceans of molten stone
pox her face, alchemists tell us.

No flowers painting the land
as when Icarus lived: magnolias,
amaryllis, and roses in dreams;
lilies, irises, and orchids in legend.

The land itself barren: obsidian
and granite crags, jagged spars
of sharp ice, cliffs, promontories,
harsh peaks of rugged mountains.

Icarus? He got his heart's desire.
His wings forever curve across
the empyrean night. His morsels
scintillate like jewels in a crown.

Gaunt

Charles Gramlich

As autumn shadows
evolve into winter nights,
hunger comes sniffing.

Gaunt, the gray wolf has grown.
With yellow eyes.
Her belly snarls a wild music of want,
to match the growl in her throat.

In the spring she fed well
from the hunt.
Her teeth left the green grass
dappled with red.

But summer came warm
and did not warm her.
Heat drove the hunted to ground.
Sickness claimed her pack.

On a hushed and lorn eve,
in a desperate famine,
through cold black woods
she came weak to my fire.

I threw her the carcass
of my feast,
and she became my muse.
In no way domesticated.

With strength returned, she hunted.
Spurning the tame food I offered,
she left me the feathers
of some gutted prey.

Now on occasion she visits.
At edge of fire and shadow,
only her eyes glow.
We judge each other warily.

We will be friends,
a pack of two.
Or one will kill the other.

Reversed Polarities

Nin Harris

1 June 2015

I have been alone before I knew what that word meant.

I drank down poems about solitude as a teenager
and savored its treacly sadness, sweet like gula melaka
and as smooth as P. Ramlee's voice wooing
a sarong-clad school teacher in black-and-white cinema.

It was a melancholy romance that cushioned the bleak blow
of surviving only on one's own limited energy reserves.

I grew adept.

I became a generator not just for myself
but for others, stray travelers and passers-by.
Generating light, warmth, and comfort.

Alone.

It was such a delicious word,
filled with sad nobility,
the taste of dark cherries
swirled with dark liquors
Hades would not turn down.

*

Solitude became less palatable one day;
it carried the bleakness of unwatered gravel.
It was an isolation that had lost the romance of salvation.

Perhaps someone would change this fundamental condition—
perhaps love or desire would transform this dynamic.
This too was a romance, too luscious for words,
like the libido-teasing scent of fingers burned by guitar strings
or lychees, drizzled with the syrup of cane sugar.

That particular flavour died the night someone taught me
that to be possessed was to witness my body
transformed into a party I was not invited to attend.

It danced its own dance while my soul remained
in a dark hall encircled by bleak mirrors;
my face staring back at me as mathematics, theoretical physics,
eternal debates circling around *a priori* versus *a posteriori*
distracted me from staring at the dance that happened,
separate from my conscious self,
constructing a textbook endorsement for
epiphenomenalism out of my profound dismay.

This too was foreordained within the confines
of black-and-white cinema.

The generator switched off.

Switching it back on required
a shift in frequency and voltage.
I learned to embrace the bleakness
and to reverse my polarities.

My generator is now fueled by dark matter
exuding enough pull to repel and to swallow universes.

Mummies

Richard Hedderman

Milwaukee Public Museum

When children ask if it's frightening
when they come alive, I tell them yes,
of course it is, it's absolutely terrifying,
and believe me, you don't want to be around

when it happens, especially at night.
When they ask if the mummies walk
with their arms outstretched like mummies
in the movies, I tell them no, it's nothing

like that. You see, I explain, the muscles
of their arms have atrophied from thousands
of years of disuse; they just can't walk
around the way mummies do in movies.

In fact, I explain, their feet have been so
lovingly and carefully bound by strips
of flax linen, that it's difficult for them
to walk at all, which explains the halting

gait, the fear that at any moment they will stumble
and pitch forward, landing in a heap of rags.
Can they talk? No, they can't talk, not after
all those years in tombs choked with the dust

of centuries and the weight of eternity
upon them. Can they see, they want to know.
Not any more, I say, for long ago
their eyes were replaced with onions or stones,

stones as white as the sun. Finally, I explain,
they long only to wander forth as they used to,
and once again admire their reflections
in the shimmering Nile of the gallery floor.

Glinda's Dilemma

Gloria Heffernan

Don't think it's easy having all the answers.
It's tough hovering just beyond your reach
in this stupid pink bubble,
barely visible but ever present,
knowing the short cut,
and knowing it won't matter a damn
unless you find your own way.

Just ask Dorothy.
Do you think she would have been so happy
to get back to those grey Kansas cornfields,
if she hadn't seen through all that technicolor glitz herself?
Yellow brick roads are nice,

but it took a few flying monkeys
for her to really believe
there's no place like home.

I could have told her right off the bat
about those ruby slippers,
but I didn't because my therapist warned me
about codependent behavior,
and said that I have to learn to let people
make their own mistakes.

Which brings me back to you
and all those lions and tigers and bears
you keep mistaking for lovers.
Imagine how I feel,
watching you going around in circles and
wanting to give you the answer,
hopelessly trying to prove to you that
the wicked witch can't hurt you anymore.

It would be so easy.
All you have to do is
click your heels three times
and say I love you.
And I will be your home.

Selenites

John Philip Johnson

Each lunar sunrise they say,
as though their world is starting over,
"Come, let us reason together,"
and off they go, but not too far off.

Reclined in craters, they utter syllogisms
to each other, love songs made of feldspar.
They trace formulae in jagged moon dust
with the tips of their tapered fingers.

They are wearing togas as though awaiting
Europeans from the Age of Enlightenment.
They are crowned by idiosyncratic mathematics.
Calm pervades their minds.

They disturb nothing. There is nothing to do.
There is no work for their bodies, nothing
to acquire. Through semi-translucent skin
with a gray sheen, they feed directly on the sun,

turning light into ongoing thought.
A few steps beyond their usual haunts lies
the pewter grit of the surface, monochromatic
and uninterrupted for a hundred million years.

Late every afternoon, their philosophy
begins its disintegration. Logic goes
to extremes; lines of thought play out.
The premises reach uncreated places.

The edifice flickers, fails, disappears.
They stash their bodies in the crevices.
Night comes upon them. Cosmic wind
blows through them. They lodge themselves,

and their posterity, in a hall of dreams,
and become like invisible fish, visiting
impossible things in black, unseen seas.
Meaning foams about them in semiotic bits.

Thoughts are rendered into proteins.
A softness overtakes their minds, like breath.
Then, when the rod of sunlight strikes,
they rise with a vague reluctance.

"Come," they say. The first argument
of the morning quickly reasons away,
and they forget who they are.

Kraken

Tim Jones

Millennia of sunlight passed the Kraken by.
He slept where he had fallen, each molecule
bound up in water ice, kept safe by permafrost
or the pressure of the deep. Kraken lay
unmoved beneath the waves, deep in his dreams
of fire and air, while the ice sat heavy on the poles
and the clever, clever apes, fizzing with language,
trudged northwards out of Africa.

Unperturbed slept Kraken as the glaciers withdrew.
Lapping at their tongues came the clever apes,
furred, speared, striding on. Wintering in caves,
they met and mated with their slow-tongued cousins,
gaining their immunities, their thicker skins.
Tinder sparked to flame in the wolf-howled night,
each tribe protected in its ring of fire,
but Kraken took no notice of such things.

Light disturbed Kraken's millennial dreams,
sunlight no longer reflected by protective ice
but slanting down into the depths, unchecked,
warming the shallow seas, permafrost
proving to be less than permanent. In his sleep,
Kraken rolled over, farted, belched. Siberia trembled,
craters forming where none had been, methane
bursting skyward across the Arctic night.

The clever apes looked, and shrugged, and looked away.
They had bigger fish to fry: death, war,
their endless clawing at the Earth for fuel. Kraken
had been banished from their world. He was a relic of myth,
terror of the Greenland Sea, muse to Tennyson,
John Wyndham antagonist, large-boned
inhabitant of green-screened Greek epics,
set free to give Perseus something to kill.

The old Norse knew his nature well. *Hafgufa*
they named him, sea steam: and so he rose,
bubbling up beneath the circumpolar seas,
so much methane rising to warm the skies
that it roused him more, the loop reinforcing,
unstoppable, his coils releasing, sea floor gaping open,
undersea landslides lashing crowded coasts with waves,
the clever apes at last obliged to pay attention—

but too late. The Kraken is awake.
Flares light the Arctic night to write his name.
His is the fire that heats the deep, that scours the land
clean of everything that flies and walks and crawls—
the few survivors, vainly fleeing south,
hearing his voice forever louder at their backs.
The Kraken roars, and as he roars
soon every trace of clever ape is burned away.

This poem refers to "The Kraken Wakes" by Alfred, Lord Tennyson (1830).

Moth and Memory

Sandra Kasturi

for Michael Rowe

Plume moths remove remembering.
Their feathery snowtouch on the eyelids
sifts out thought and will,
leavens facts until they rise
into the air and pop
into oblivion.

Moths' delicate footprints
on the skin, invisible
as sorrows, chase away
longing and desire, chase
knowledge of things.
Of self, of trees and acorns,
glass jars, death and daisies,
gazelles and geodes.

All of it, gone.

Until we are blank, unfurrowed,
smoothed right out of our lives,
scooped out like a hollowed melon.
Moths whirling around our heads,
a petal-storm of white hawthorn,
each flick of wing counting
back, removing month, day, minute,
unravelling selves and selvages.

Knowledge of moths, too,
goes in the end. The final thing
to slip away; the last
touch we feel: moths'
shivery tickle on our bodies
become meaningless.

Say goodbye now, before moth
and memory give way to air.
Say, farewell Death's Head, fare-
well Emperor, Luna, Elephant Hawk.
Polyphemus. Io. Mottled Beauty.
Memory, goodbye. Plume moth
mottled memory, goodbye.

Venice Letting Go

Sandra Kasturi

It was like Venice letting go of the pretense of being attached to land.
—from "The Vervain" by David Keyes, *I Do So Worry for All Those Lost at Sea*

Let go of the carnival,
dark dear heart,
the old familiar masques
and marauders, the dredged
canals of the mooniest
reflected moon. Let go
the bilge pumps
and the gaudy gondolas.
Raise each finger gently
from the edges of land
and float away, Venice—
drift toward the great-finned
open sea, with its sawtoothed
mermaids and its saltlick
heart. Drift away
from the resolutions of soil,
the firmness of tree roots
and terraces. Slip away
from your sinking. Comb
through the tangled limbs
of kraken and cuttlefish.
Drink from mollusc shells
and send telephone messages
by conch or albatross. Toss
your knives and forks overboard
and use only tridents for eating.
Let go of your attachments,
Venice, dear Venice. Leave
behind the rigours of fences
and borders. Take your ancient
palazzos and antique linens,
your dusty wine bottles
and red glass goblets
and say a final farewell
to land. Become
the iridescent bubble dream
on the wavecap, the pop
of gilded fairytale foam
you were always meant to be.

hard copy

Herb Kauderer

Steinwachs can't remember
how he became so dependent
on Luna City's Secret Society
of the Written Word

but he can see that they own him
now & he accepts his position
smuggling hydroponics & printers
& infocubes

all in exchange
for a steady trickle of rough
hemp-paper printouts folded &
bound into secret chronicles

that somehow remain completely
untraceable to
electronic authorities
incapable of unplugging

and in the margins
of his favorite folios
he haltingly adds
his own story

luddite's dream

Herb Kauderer

victrola days defy
radiant nights

whisper lies
in dreamland

blow bubbles
of times & ages

encase sleep in
measured spheres

cleansed of wildness
devoid of danger

floating through
the nuclear haze
at ease

The Changeling's Gambit

Sasha Kim

they don't tell you
the circle of mushrooms may as well
be inevitable

seasons will choke,
leaving husks dense
with regret

they don't tell you
to save yourself: you must be willing
to succumb to the pull

drowning is not so easy
as gulping water
or falling

listen

it does not matter where you step:
outcomes are different
than conclusions

your surrender:
affirmation
recourse

and perhaps when your lungs flood
with regret
and the surge of air wrests away
your pauses

you will be redeemed:

infinite circles
never unravel

Deborah P Kolodji

re-entry heat
he spends the night
on the couch

The Only Time Machine

David C. Kopaska-Merkel

We upload your consciousness,
it runs in a simulated 1960s Lagos,
the quaint elder city;
but it's totally cool!
OK, it runs slowly,
and it's grainy (a few details are lacking),
but the Uploaded never notice; they lack detail too.

Your body is destroyed in the process,
but it's immortality; don't worry,
we keep you backed up,
we have uninterruptible power supplies,
backups on our backups,
real-time monitoring of conditions on the drive,
and if you do get corrupted,
you never know it!

It's the perfect existence,
and the only way to go back in time.

Yes, Lagos–60s™ is the best and only,
although I hear someone is about to launch
a goth sim called Bombardment 1851,
which is supposed to really rock,
if you're into that sort of thing;
but, for a small fee,
we can make a copy of you for that platform,
to upload when they go live.

Rip Van Winkle On Mars

David C. Kopaska-Merkel

I'd dreamed a Martian tundra:
tussocks, tiny flowers—
I guess I overslept

Dome open to the thin cold sky,
rooms agape, no thing left behind,
a burn mark where the lander crouched
is their goodbye

out back a midden: wrappers, boxes;
hunkering, I see a bit of gray-green mold
inside a plastic wrap,
company is good, but for companionship
I'll need to wait a few billion years.

I *could* use a nap.

Post-Apocalyptic Toothbrush

Betsy Ladyzhets

They left you dangling on the edge of the counter, bristles still damp,
left you as they packed up cans and boxes, flashlights and clubs,
left you just where you could hear the shrieks echoing off tiled walls—
but not *quite* where you could catch a glimpse of beasts in the mirror.

And the boys invaded in ski masks, combed through every inch,
took sweaters and silverware and red Solo cups,
bulldozers determined to leave no stain of human existence—
when they tore through the bathroom, they stole all your friends.

"Wait!" you wanted to shout. "Take me! I have Crest Whitening,
and I'm guaranteed to exterminate plaque! Don't you know
I'm recommended by five out of six dentists?"

Where are the dentists now?

Ode to Dorothy Gale

Jenna Lê

Tell me, O muse,
of L. Frank Baum's naïf:
like Odysseus,
she suffered homesickness and grief.

Like Odysseus,
the home she pined for was a farm.
She wore a farm girl's dress.
She swung a basket on her arm.

Like Odysseus,
she led a straggling ragtag crew.
Odysseus's friends plied wooden oars.
Miss Gale's friends buffed her ruby shoes.

Decked in pleats and plaits,
ensnarled by plot and plight,
she plodded and she pleaded
through the cyclone-upturned night.

She pled for favors from
a band of witches, fairy sprites.
She coaxed the pink one, "Help me home!"
She begged the green one, "Spare my life!"

But Odysseus
behaved no differently.
He coaxed fair Circe, "Kiss my lips!"
He begged Calypso, "Mount my knee!"

Odysseus wiped
the smug look from a cyclops's face.
Dorothy put
a fraudulent wizard in his place.

Starry eyes framed by
a pair of glossy tassels,
Miss Gale prevailed, acclaimed by
her straw-made, tin-made, leonine vassals.

I didn't read the *Odyssey*
until I was sixteen.
It was the film *The Wizard of Oz*
that shaped my childhood dreams:

Dorothy's epic song
taught me, another Midwest kid,
that even a neglected orphaned long-
haired girl can't bid

adieu to Kansas,
adieu to Ithacan fields,
without a backward glance, and backward glances
never heal.

Flora and Fauna

James Frederick Leach

In Father Cochran's "Forest Memoir,"
the ragged, hirsute bard recalls
Spring's most vicious signal:
the yellow noses of the Flower Wolves.

A local vegetation grew,
dubbed the "Deadman's Pantaloons,"
brightly colored, reeking of the grave,
its nectar laced with entheogen.

Scavengers, winter-starved,
eager for carrion, were drawn
by its scent to the hidden sylvan copses,
lured to these beds of necrotic narcotic.

Razor bears, Hook-Beak Crows,
Ebony Vultures, of course,
but the region's apex predator
was a clan of *Canis floridus*.

Cochran retired to these woods
to track this rare fraternity
and recount in verse their feral congress.
Only fragments of his sojourn survive.

The recluse's most beloved lyric
mimicks the raucous chorus
of these unruly, blossom-drunk beasts
and relates their vernal ritual, their passion.

These strange dogs worshipped the plants,
thrusting snouts amid the petals,

rolling, paws curled in ecstasy,
cavorting like frenzied religion.

Poets, it's said, are kin to the dog
and Cochran perhaps more than most.
That mad enthusiast gladly joined
their canine rite, their holy howling.

His songs also lapse from scansion,
revert to syllables, most uncivil.
(It's whispered of his impious inspirations,
"His Muse descended when the Moon rose.")

He never revised his unkempt lines.
Archers found his abandoned notes
while culling myth-worthy game,
their shafts equipped with silver tips.

I've roamed in vain through Cochran's woods,
sniffed the air for decay, seeking
his golden, death-scented bloom.
Its balm, alas, is quite extinct.

Its existence would trouble our secular age.
Not the delusion-inducing elixir, rather
the plant itself, apparently pollinated
by the play of rural lycanthropes.

The Dreaded Dreadnoughtus

B.J. Lee

We played in the forest
of Gondwana-Horus.
We sought the Dreadnoughtus,
the titanosaurus.

With swagger and haught-us,
we sought the Dreadnoughtus.
With swords for the onslaught,
we sought the Dreadnoughtus.

We saw the Dreadnoughtus,
that horrid old saurus.
He stood in the forest.
Ah! How he awed us!

He turned and he saw us.
He didn't care for us.
He made a great roar-us.
We screamed in a chorus.

We ran lest he paw us
or claw us or gnaw us.
We ran through the forest
of Gondwana-Horus.

We outran the saurus,
relieved to the core-us!
We beat the Dreadnoughtus,
that naughty old saurus.

But Dreadnoughtus taught us
to not be so haught-us,
or play in the forest
of Gondwana-Horus.

The Washerwoman's Daughter

Mary Soon Lee

barefoot, down by the river,
hauling water, rinsing clothes,
she's kissed a thousand frogs

moist, faintly slimy,
their eyes bulging at her
as she lifts them

but not one prince among them,
and why hope for a prince
in the first place?

to live among foreigners
and have someone else
wash her clothes for her?

only there is something
she wants, something that
swells in her like sadness

when she sees her mother,
red-handed, wrinkled,
still kissing frogs.

B'resheet

Julia Burns Liberman

This is how it was for Lilith, first-born
human daughter of the Lord, first wife
to a man whose name was mud:

She was born into the orgasm of life,
the entire world stroking her towards devotion.
Thereafter, she spent the rest of her existence
searching for the exaltation of her first breath.

She thought that Adam had felt it too—that he
recalled the rapturous breath of God upon his skin,
remembered standing in the glory of Creation,
filled with the ecstasy of living. She hoped
that together they might reassemble
enough parts to make the whole of it,
to recreate the awe of entering the universe.

But he did not know, and he did not remember,
and his idea of pleasure was so small it bored her.
And that was why she had left Adam and the Garden
behind: he did not remember the feeling,
any more than he could redeliver it.

Every time she returns to Eden, after years
of searching for slivers of satisfaction, she sits
beneath the Tree of Knowledge. She touches
herself, eating of its many fruits: peaches, mangoes,
pomegranates, and figs. She is trying to find
the one that will teach her how to return
to the Beginning.

Postlude

Nolan Liebert

The human swansong is radioactive,
bleeding out the afterlife
in decay
of full-bodied isotopes,
of thin-bodied corpses,
of animal bones

touched by the godforce
of a single metal raindrop—

it was pewter-colored cancer
growing on the face of the sky,
screaming
toward the ground—

a requiem
of light and the darkness of tombs
marked by untouched dinner plates
and interlocked knots of skeletons,
marked by flowers on rooftops
and deer grazing in the living room,
marked by snowing statues of ash
forever in the middle of something.

An Introduction to Alternate Universes: Theory and Practice

Sandra J. Lindow

> *Our Universe is just one among very many "bubble universes," all popping out of the general medium of the Big Bang like bubbles forming in a glass of beer. Somewhere perhaps there are many universes more or less like ours, some very similar to and others radically different from the universe we call "home."*
> —John G. Cramer "Other Universes II," *Analog* 11/84

I. Universal Soup

Inside the dark cauldron
universes bubble,
each bubble emerging,
breaking, becoming twinned—
"Double, double toil and trouble"
when life begins within.

II. Universal Tree

A time tree of universes
rooted in Ygdrasil,
formed by branching possibilities,
the crotch of each branch,
a crisis where time splits,
heralded by the crow, "What If?"

III. Dream Door

A microcosm of macro universes
in the shiny veneer,
wood of would,
the lintel is a shibboleth;
a handle the size of a sonnet
opens to a dreamer's kiss.

IV. What If?

Somewhere onions dream,
whales sing oratorio; Elvis lives.
Universes not yet conceived
quicken behind the medulla oblongata,
providing magic starship rides
into alternate possibilities,
but getting home is tricky.

V. The Glass

Is cold,
I take a sip.

Under the Cancer Tree

Sandra J. Lindow

At the foot of the Cancer Tree
is a cave where reside three women:
one sews, one rips, one chooses.
They pass a single eye and ear

between them. At any one time
only one can see, one can hear:
one ear to hear the silent prayers,
one eye to see the broken.

Only the one both deaf and blind
will choose—
a committee's lack of responsibility
for the fallen.

No one can meet them
and come away unshaken.

Four Chambers

Shira Lipkin

This is not the heart
I would have chosen to give you,
this ragged thing
with topographical scars
like splayed hands,
like exposed nerves—
trace me, map me
learn the places I was flayed open,
learn how I saved myself.

This is me,
four rounds chambered.
Those scars, they call them rifling
unique as a heart;
you'd know me anywhere,
my scars, my words
my songs—
in the heart of your chamber,
hum,
and I'm your resonant frequency,
your sonic shadow.

Listen: I have room for you.
Every time I've torn I've grown.
Rifle through me,
await the ruling,
I'll wait; I will sing your way in.

Challenger

Bronwyn Lovell

Ascending for seventy-three euphoric
seconds we thought they'd got away.

A second sun bloomed in the sky,
eruption eclipsed our ears and I don't

know whether that whine was spiralling
rockets or a collective scream but I do know

it was the worst sound to ever howl through
me. Later, I learned the crew must've survived

initially, though it would have been kinder
if they'd died in the blast. The cabin went

ballistic—traced a perfect rainbow
to its fool's gold end. Rudderless

and wingless for two-and-three-quarter
minutes' eternity the crew was conscious,

toggling switches in vain. Comms down.
Power out. Recorder stopped. Oxygen on.

Hell, they could see death coming,
but had no way to stop it and no one to tell.

It Came to Pass

Mark Mansfield

In memory of Edward O. Knowlton

Psychics, predictably, became about as common as enchanted oaks
in Elf Town.
From Stonehenge to Roswell,
epiphanies multiplied faster than jackrabbits.
Herbalists outearned Wall Street.
Wind chimes and clearly marked runes were required by law.
Séances and crystal-gazing replaced mandatory schooling,
and soon, no one dared admit to not having lived
at least one previous life.

Constantly dogged by the intuitive goon squads,
the last few linear thinkers cast themselves out.
Forced to subsist on near-brainstorms and semi-
valid syllogisms, they hid inside the vacant classrooms,
boarded-up laboratories, and condemned libraries
where sometimes late at night while reasoning in whispers,
they would hear the stag hoofs
or glimpse its silver mane, or lion's tail
in the clear light cast down the darkened halls

from its single horn as it stood there, listening.

The Subtle Arts of Chemistry

Elizabeth R. McClellan

Dance the benzene ring around,
whirling six times three—

trace Lewis dot sigils in quicksilver,
ionic bond prisons for errant souls.

Mendeleev's sacred alphabet hides
a multiplicity of gods, one hundred
eighteen abbreviated divinities.

Write their names on your heart
in columns ordered by gravitas.

Beware the so-called noble gases.
Aloof, they cannot be trusted
to aid when you call. Put your faith

in earthly things—carbon, oxygen,
hydrogen and helium, sun and starlight,
knowing you are already liquid
by nature though solid in form,
perhaps to sublimate someday.

Titrate glucol and atropa belladonna
drop by drop into a solution
of artemesia absinthium.

Note the moon and the lady
in your lab notebook,
the subtle changes in the green.

Dream of sailing
natural satellite seas,
a basalt summer cottage
on the shores of Mare Imbrium,

guide your meditations
toward the Technicolor advent
of distant stars, birthed
from the dust-cloud of your regrets.

The Woman Sings Her Marriage Into Being

Lev Mirov

Hear, O Desert: I am returning to the place where I was born.
Back to the barrow-hills, where scarlet birds nest among the mounds of the dead
to claim my bride and ransom her into the land of the living.
I shall lay down my ancestral sword, and bare my head before God and the moon
I shall prepare a wedding feast with my own two hands
bread as flat and round as a silver coin to buy entry into the land of death
wine made sweet with the passage of time, poured out on the earth
the perfumed fat of young goats to burn in the bone-fire.
When the birds roost above me, and look down upon my marriage feast
I shall summon forth the wife I have long loved:
the drum shall sound my heartbeat, endless repeating
the sound of God's steps dancing the world into being.
I shall raise my voice, and sing the song of life
which raised the first body from the dust long ago.
My hands will crack and open, and by blood prove my devotion.
Down she will come from among the towers, my scarlet bird with a woman's voice
and I will dance, red skirts sweeping the mud I have made.
For her I will show the pattern of the living, all the things we shall have together:
the wind, ours to outrun, the moon, to guide our path, the river, to water our souls
the fields of my father, the herds of my mother, all the things we will inherit
the life appointed to me by the stars above. Mine, but no more mine alone.
And out of love for me, the singing bird, my crimson lover,
shall wear a woman's face to be my wife, a mask pulled from the many shapes of
        the moon
to have a life in flesh once again and return with me to where the living dwell.
Hear, O Desert: at dawn, two will leave the place of the dead beneath the sun.
I am bringing my wife into the world.

Bone-House

A.J. Odasso

Your beauty wounds me still,
your words sunk thorn-sharp
in my marrow. You're a vice
I never gave up, no matter

what I may claim when my lover
pries. *Hús-bónd*, house-bound

to blood and bone my heart
has been, but not to home.

Your eyes, bright-weft, my brick
and mortar, your quick mind
my only thrill.

Transition Metal

A.J. Odasso

I learned metals early. My uncle,
a jeweler, garlanded his mother

in gold. My grandmother's rings
held diamond, topaz, and garnet

too costly for words. At nine,
she fitted a circlet, silver, set

with blood-flecked carbon
on my little finger. I grew

till I had to thread it through
that cheap herringbone chain

a hopeful beau gave me. Kiss
girls after sundown and no-one

will see you wear moonlight
where others insist you don sun.

In Fits of Wildest Dreaming

K. A. Opperman

In fits of wildest dreaming,
When demons all were teeming,
And scheming
To conquer midnight's throne,
I tossed in deepest slumber,
Through nightmares without number,
To cumber
The more, with awful groan,

My bed of silken scarlet.
A harpy-wingèd harlot—
A starlet
From courts of white Selene—
Seemed hellishly to hover
About me like a lover,
And cover,
With kisses so obscene,

My body, helpless sleeping!—
It seemed that she was reaping,
And keeping,
My soul with every kiss!
The succubus embraced me,
In ghostly beauty faced me,
To taste me,
And let me dream of bliss.

But there was scarce of pleasure,
No amorous red measure
To treasure,
Within my poisoned pulse;
For restless woes and worries
Swirled round me like lemures,
Or flurries
Of leaves that soon convulse

In graying autumn grasses,
As pensively there passes
Of lasses
The saddest of them all—
Poor Vespertina's specter,
When purple dusk has decked her,
Her nectar
Gone all to bitter gall.

And all the ghouls were howling,
The moonlit tombs befouling—
An owling
Made much of mournful moan—
When I was wildly dreaming,
And demons all were teeming,
And scheming
To conquer midnight's throne.

The Palace of Phantasies

K. A. Opperman

I have a little time upon my couch to lie;
    Therefore this eve I give unto the vagaries—
    The purple phantasies—
Of my imagination's daemon, soaring high
On fragrant censer smoke and my escaping sigh,
    Ennui awhile to ease.

Enthroned on crimson cushions deep with pillows piled,
    Encrowned with drowsiness, I rule a dim demesne
    Where opium, not pain,
Presides over a palace opulent, enisled
By suffering and sadness, yet still undefiled
    By their besieging stain.

But now a hushed unrest has crept into its halls;
    Voices of evil hiss behind each arras fair;
    Vermiculate, the vair;
The shadows cast by candles spread like creeping palls;
The chalice wherefrom I would quaff rare magistrals
    Conium seems to bear.

Even into my deepest keep a plague pursues—
    Even up to the crowning tower's highest heights.
    I tire of the delights
Illusory in which I thought myself to lose;
My house of spectral pleasures quakes as Boredom brews—
    For whims the worst of blights.

I sit as king within a crumbling empery,
    Abandoned by my subjects, facing monstrous doom,
    My marble throne, my tomb.
Too soon the towers builded so fantastically
Against my worldly weariness descend with me
    Through dead and dreamless gloom.

I wake upon my crimson couch—the hour is late;
    The censer is extinguished, and its coals are cold
    Within its figured gold.
Alas, my daemon listless lies where once it sate
With wings outspread to prove the vesper's violet gate—
    Which now no more unfold.

Requiem

Matt Quinn

Alone upon the surface of the moon,
a spaceman weeps. His helmet fills with tears
that form a sea to mock this man marooned
on barren rock. These thirteen airless years

now weigh upon his lungs with gravities
far greater than the moon's. In the dark sky
of lunar night, the Earth is all he sees,
still smouldering its terminal goodbye.

The tears now penetrate into his suit,
electric circuits short out, start to spark.
His inter-planet radio, long mute,
blasts bursts of broken static from the dark,

as radiation from the distant Earth
is amplified by saline-coated wires.
The whining discord of white noise gives birth
to softer, subtler tones that now acquire

a melancholy hue and seem to whisper
fragments of some long-forgotten song.
The static falls away, the sound grows crisper;
a ghostly signal sings out clear and strong.

Unearthly violins eke out a theme
that's then reprised by instruments unknown;
ethereal timbres stolen from his dreams
unite to sculpt a blue-green world of tone.

The music conjures smells of fresh-baked bread
and new-mown hay, then visions of the farm
his parents had, the church in which he wed.
He sees his bride release her father's arm.

A shift of scene: his daughter's laughter spills
in soft glissandos, catches winds that lift
a bread-bag kite above the sheep-grazed hills.
He weeps again, so grateful for this gift

of cosmic sound that's conjured up the shades
of those he loves. The ending comes too soon.
As static breaks back in, the music fades.
His mirage dims. He's pulled back to the moon.

And so he weeps again, but this time cries
as if to drown a world, can't stand to face
the darkness twice, as everybody dies
once more, and he's left emptier than space.

Lola

Gabby Reed

My grandmother climbed the balete tree and disappeared
forever. There, where the branches are draped in themselves,
the tree that roots in the air. Where nobody could tell her
what was real or unreal, nobody could say that a sound wasn't
there. Climbed the balete into the under-husk of the world where
everything exists. And I am scared that one day I will make the climb,
that I will hear them too, that they were always there. My skin
will peel back like summer bark, and I will find roots among my hair.

Attack of The Saurus

John Reinhart

The dictionaries cower in fear
while the complete Shakespeare
runs for cover behind the less nimble
classical texts in Greek.
Modern poetry babbles incoherently,
even the no-nonsense nonfiction
was unprepared for this rabid
assault, attack, barrage, battle, battery,
charge, duel, fight, fracas, joust,
melée, offensive, onslaught, siege,
from the previously, until now, earlier,
erstwhile friendly, content, happy,
nice, passive, pleasant, polite, tame,
timid thesaurus.

Lot's Wife

Michelle Scalise

They forced her into the future
letting it tear her to shreds
before she could blink away
what was to come.
What she wouldn't forget
if they stoned her to death.
A world without light
to keep the demons at bay,
more evil than anything
she'd screamed about in nightmares.
"Look ahead," she was warned by
faces blank as sheets of parchment.
A belt around her neck
pulling her into fate.
Her eyes sewn open,
Dry as the desert.
"This is your tomorrow,"
But the truth was louder than their god.
There was no sun before her,
just shadows so gray
a beam of light couldn't labor through.
Sand turning to snow,
wind kissing her lips until they bled.
Fingers turned to brittle bones
Until her ring slid off with her skin.
"Hurry!" they cried
dragging her closer to a room
without doors,
without hope.
Breaking free she knelt to the image of yesterday
drowning in her own sea of salt and tears.

He Promised Me The Moon

Marge Simon

I came here hoping
this world would suffice,
but all I met were flimsy ghosts

playing with fractals and logistics,
as meaningless as gossip—until him.

He hired me as his model,
even promised me the moon
before his wife's death.
I wasn't planning on this,
to know such *human* feelings.

He begged me to move in, after.
But he sits now, staring at his paintings.
He won't even let me touch him.
Her flowers shrivel in their pots,
for want of her special love.

She was from Orlando,
a crowded, touristy place
of slender women, cocktails
at four, fashion-wise and empty-
headed as the rest of their lot.

But I don't leave him. I can't.
It makes me wince, knowing
I can assume a liquid form,
a creature foreign to this world,
from a planet of endless storms.

Perhaps tomorrow he'll be aware,
pick up his palette, have me pose.
I don't care how painful or how long,
I only want him to undress me,
kiss me in familiar places—

I'll find us a moon of our own,
far from Earth.

Serving the Blind Girl

Marge Simon

The pigeons moan when the blind girl calls,
for she is hungry and will be wanting pigeon pie.

Eugene sits in his big yellow chair to polish his spike.
I watch as he brushes the chamois over the walnut pole
until his fingers are stained darker than his skin.

We try to please her with small things, whatever we can manage.
I am embroidering a pillow for her with lilies that she can touch
on the surface of the rough cloth, perhaps even feel their color.

The blind girl is the last of her kind but she is not a witch,
not those poor creatures that were burned or drowned.
She calls us in visions when our services are needed
to purify our flock, and graciously we comply.

We are hers to bid, as a mother would bid her children,
and not a one of us dares question her except for fools
such as Rafe, misshapen and foul-mouthed, often drunk.
So it was natural that his blaspheming head wound up
on the sharp end of Eugene's pole, supper for the crows.

There is always a great feasting and celebration
whenever a head finds its way to the spike,
when the blind girl calls.

Before I Kill You (An Arch-Villainelle)

David Sklar

Although I'm not particularly vain,
I'm sure you'd like to know how you will die,
so, first, before I kill you, I'll explain

my brilliant plan. Don't bother to complain;
you won't escape, no matter how you try.
It's not that I'm particularly vain,

it's just that after taking all these pains
I would like you to look me in the eye
before I kill you, so I can explain:

a cistern in the mountain gathers rain
through ducts in my enormous statue's eye
(not that I am particularly vain).

It enters a robotic water main,
which, on command, can self-electrify.
Before I kill you, now, I will explain:

I've added some enhancements to my brain—
you'll nev— What's that? You're out? Good grief! Good bye;
good riddance. It's a good thing I'm not vain;
next time, before I kill you, I'll explain.

The Case of Trying Too Hard

Steve Sneyd

Each case turns on its own facts
The incident where eyes were pulled out to eat
Having no provable connection whatsoever
With the Gibbet Street case of the squinched-up house

Citizens can be more sure
That we keep records of every dubious occurrence
That so far not the trace of a pattern has emerged
Despite endless manual and computer cross-analysis

That there is no need for alarm: indeed
Statistically the incidence is far less
Than of stars blowing up in outer space
And none of us worry our heads about them, do we?

The spokesman ceases and the DJ
Puts on Sweet Poison 'Itching on a Dime'—
Immensity of hairy slime, the monster
Welcomes the excuse for ceasing what it's doing

Chewing a new-born baby in a sandwich of skinned womb
To ponder with vague unformed sadness
Why knowing what you do is wrong will never
Help you stop and change your nature

Squirming like rat on hook the watching father
Wished his heart would stop
His impotence to help to save his own against
The crouch of malformation filling what had been 3 rooms

Finishing the last soft-bone nibble of its snack
The creature pondered shaplessly why just like Marilyn
Monroe endlessly impossibly failing to be understood
It could not ever get its need its pain its dreams across

Pulped the man's head one-pawed leaving
Tunnelling back to sewererd earth to deep safe den
To where it would attempt again like a materialising medium
Straining to summon out of chaos something up to love

raven speaks

Michael Spring

if I get the chance I'll split your eye in two
my beak will snap and clack after each fleeting half

your eye will become two then four then eight
your other eye will float above, witnessing
a storm of shadow, a whirlwind of light

if I get the chance I'll crack open your head
for you to capture the subtle pitches
and timbres from trees

along with the thrumming of the earthworm
and the drumming of the sphinx moth

you need me often in your life, but not always
when you want me

many times, like now, I'll be ravenous
to cut something from you

you might say my feathers are blackened from creation
or burnt after stealing the sun
I won't deny this—I'm multiple
just as my colors are compressed
into what you perceive as black

you will see only what you can see
but that is why I'm here:
creating bones for clouds,
caves from stars

with black mirrors for eyes

David Lee Summers

buried pet turtles
by moonlight
shelled zombies arise

Origami Crane/Light-Defying Spaceship

Naru Dames Sundar

Origami crane with big spaceship dreams,
Crisp Japanese paper painted in peonies
Creased into feather and bone and
The absence of feet, with soft bloated corners.
(*Because the boy*
    with his toffee-sticky fat fingers
        was impatient)

But mountain and valley are not fusion torii
And the field of peonies does not limn starlight.
Marooned on the faded mahogany table
With no hope of sky, dreaming of
Astrogation, nebulae, and the gleam of suns

In its deep paper heart, lantern-bright,
Folds turn into spars, and valleys into engines
And origami crane skitters across galaxies.

[*This poem is intended to be read as two parallel columns.*]

Light-defying spaceship with tiny paper dreams,
City-long spars of iron painted in somber gray,
Tessellated into hull and spine and
Geometries sculpted by dead mathematicians.
(*Because shipwrights*
with their coffee-stained hands
abjure ornament and gilt)

But bones of steel are not creases like blades,
And ten clicks of engine do not fit on a single page.
Adrift in the empty, beyond well and orbit,
With no hope of simple pleasures, dreaming of
Mountain, valley, edge and fold.

In its sad metal-clad heart, molten as suns,
Spars turn to folds, and engines into valleys
And light-defying spaceship collapses into a

Tiny yellowed crane, peonies faded,
On a shipwright's table.

Philomela in Seven Movements

Natalia Theodoridou

On Mondays, she is a bird.
She feeds him her egg, sunny side up and runny.
"It's yummy," he says. "You should make this more often."

On Tuesdays, she is a tree.
Trees speak. Their stories have no verbs. They say, over and over:
"My leaves. My trunk. The air. The birds. The light. The earth. My leaves.
    My leaves. My leaves."

On Wednesdays, her smile is stuck to the back of her head.
She walks around scaring people.

On Thursdays, she stays in
with a bad case of wandering womb.

On Fridays, her skirt floats around her
like a mournful sail in the Aegean.
"Who died?" he teases.

On Saturdays, she is a continent.
"Only you and I here, my love," she says. "Your axe and my wound.
My love, my love."

On Sundays, she forgets her name.
She thinks she's a bird,
and sings.

An Unrequited Process Loops

Marie Vibbert

Love is just a chemical in the brain,
Outside the frame of the electronic.
But if its magic is merely autonomic,
Why do I feel this unrobotly pain?

Easily mocked, this fault-stopped strain,
To call it heart-break would be ironic –
Love is just a chemical in the brain,
Outside the realm of the electronic.

Whiles, ifs, untils trap me in this refrain,
My need for you is a loop that's chronic.

Why should my lithium cells all drain,
If love is just a chemical in the brain,
Outside the frame of the electronic?

The Sun Ships

Steven Withrow

Of the third of the three sun ships—
Rappahannock—only data remained,
Hieroglyphs siphoned off a fuse tube
For flight analysts' consumption.
After the *Porcupine* imploded
And the mighty *Susquehanna* met
Her incendiary demise, the eyes
Of seven solar systems opened
To the possibility of defeat.
The stars are not ours to cross,
The Nikkto diplomats intoned.
And we, dregs of the coal worlds,
Would not finance another puncture run
Even for voting rights. What blights
And bombardments had emboldened us,
And what glorious horrors had deranged
The *Rappahannock's* captain, who
Preserved in her voice log this riddle:
Teeth of fire, bands of black black black
Along the middle … devourer devourer …
The shadow tongues its fangs … why—
Before total silence consumed her.
We had a song about such creatures,
A lullaby for our babies, melodious
But meant to ward off nightmares,
So also mine-dark. The mines:
They were the sources of our fears,
They were the swallowers of light,
They were the toothed and hollow
Devourers of our hours. No shame
To sing of monsters when our home
Shot through with black black black
To the carved-out core. What's more,
We had no song for dying, we had
No mourning-song for death. We,
Like the sun ship *Rappahannock*,

Dove straight into a coal-black hole,
As Nikkto lancers split the ground,
And down down down we drowned.
The stars were not ours to cross.
The stars were not ours to cross.

Crater Conundrum Pizza

Greer Woodward

delivery to your habitat
all-terrain rover fleet
Time Toss® for msec arrival
Double Time Toss® for yesterday drop-off*
free breadsticks

*prepay required

Passenger Seat

Stephanie M. Wytovich

I've noticed lately that when I'm driving, my mind kind of blanks out, kind of goes black, and I'm drifting, drifting on the road, drifting through life and I don't even have the energy to light my cigarette, so it just hangs out my mouth as the taste of nicotine sits on my tongue, reminding me of how you used to taste, how you used to kiss me when you'd had too much wine and didn't know what you were doing, and part of me misses the uncertainty in the way you used hold me, part of me misses the way you used to look at me all scared and unsure, how you'd whisper 'you're beautiful' as if it was the most terrifying thing you'd ever said, and I've missed my street twice now thinking about you, thinking about your lips and the softness of the words you left me with, and I wonder where you are and if you're driving, if you're missing roads and running stop signs, if you're watching the stars and staying up till dawn so you can watch the darkness fade away and I've noticed lately that when I'm driving, that the music doesn't sound the same without you, that the car feels kind of empty, and the passenger seat sometimes screams.

Long Poems First Published in 2015

Toujours Il Coûte Trop Cher

Mike Allen & C.S.E. Cooney

*"In the time of Shakespeare, Joan of Arc was accepted in England as a symbol
for everything vile. He makes her out not only as a sorceress, but a charlatan
and a hypocrite; and on top of that a coward, a liar and a common slut. I
suspect they began to whitewash her when they decided that she was a virgin,
that is a sexually deranged, or at least incomplete, animal, but the idea has
always got people going, as any student of religion knows. Anyway, her stock
went up to the point of canonization. Gilles de Rais, on the other hand, is
equally a household word for monstrous vices and crimes. So much so, that he
is even confused with the fabulous figure of Bluebeard, of whom, even were he
real, we know nothing much beyond that he reacted in the most manly way to
the problem of domestic infelicity... I think, then, it is not altogether unfair to
assume that Gilles de Rais was to a large extent the victim of Catholic logic.
Catholic logic: and the foul wish-phantasms generated of its repressions, and of
its fear and ignorance. He wanted to confer a boon on humanity; therefore he
consorted with the learned; therefore he murdered little children."*
—Aleister Crowley

1. Gilles

Once I slept on satin. Now it's rat shit and straw,
goose-down pillows now piss-stained stone.
They told me they'd hang me from hooks if I didn't
confess to those lies, confess to dangling those boys,
strangling those boys, slitting those boys
and pulling out their innards, treating them as toys,
making them watch as I pulled them apart,
sitting on their stomachs and turning them blue,
watching veins bulge and burst as I ... as I ... as I ...
but none of it true! None of it! None! I am no sadist, no Satanist,
no pederast, I am none of these things, I am favored
of the King, Marshall of France, I have spilled the blood of filthy islanders
across mile after mile to restore the glory of the throne!
But they thrust prongs and heated tongs in my face,
told me, move my tongue or die without one,
promised torture to me if I did not admit torture,
pledged to sever my soul from Heaven if I did not give the Church
the false perversions it demanded. The Bishop, in his greed,
wants my manse, my lands, my title deeds, and if I must lose them, let it be!
But You, whose light, whose holy glow is surely that

I see through the slat in this forsaken door,
You must know what truth beats in my heart,
which will drop with me through the trap door in the morn
and snap when my neck cracks from my shoulders. Yes, You.
This light that shows me every granule of dust in this cell
could never come from the moon, not down here, not so removed.
O, Father, if it is You, grant miracles, spring the lock,
or grant me last sleep and escape to Paradise!
Let this luster be the last I ever see in this place!

2. Jeanne

Chevalier, at ease! The Maid is here, your Jeanne,
your friend, it's been too many years, monsieur.
Your beard is long, your skin is loose, you smell as rank as I did
after weeks in Vermandois. But never mind!
How sweet to see you, looking up at me like that, as if I were
a light, a torch, a corpse burned thrice to prove my heresy—but pardon me—
of course you were not there! One forgets.
Do you regret those days, Chevalier? Or did you cast my memory
like ash into the Seine? I've heard so much about you in the interim:
alchemy, sodomy, theatrical productions, an attempt or more to raise
a demon, and now—your own execution! Another thing we have in common.
Is it comfort you seek, my comrade, my companion in arms?
Absolution? Veneration? Shall I kiss these weeping holes that
yesterday were fingernails, these wounds that bled confession
to deeds so dark they must be writ in blood?
Shall I change your sores to jewels, promise you a life eternal
at my side, beneath my banner, haloed, holy
with cherubim to diddle daily while seraphic fiddlers play?
Is this what you wish from me, Gilles de Rais?

3. Gilles

What mad sorcery curls its fumes before my eyes?
This light you wear, it shines, swims behind your skin,
your face a lantern … you shimmer like a stained glass saint,
which you, crazed witch, could no more be than I
Lord of the Fairie Mounds. No Christian prayer of mine
could draw *you* as an answer. For damned Jeanne,
no Resurrection! This is no alchemy, no silly piddling
in fool's gold, this is evil beyond measure—Father,
O, Father, sweep aside this creature,
this luminescent shade of a madwoman …
Fraud in life and death! Fell devils spoke in many tongues
on the stage of your broken mind, their fervor stoking that glow

so magnetizing in your eyes, but it was my lone voice
won your campaigns. One more whisper in your head
but this one in your ear, to direct a mind pliant as butter.
Those armies behind you, gullible men eager for divine favor,
but it was I that engineered all your battlefield glory.

Father! Hear me! I have always been Your hand.
My blade drank soldiers, not children, emptied only deserving men
and more deserving cowards. I know no angel stands before me.
Tis a last wile of that heinous bishop, to send
this Jeanne in effigy, blazing brighter than she did even in death.
This cannot be a thing of yours, Lord. Make it not be!

4. Jeanne

I cry your pardon, *cher seigneur!*
Of course *you* know what's holy, what is pure,
you who've muttered all the Mass of Saint Sécair
from aft to fore, who've drunk deep of the waters
of the drowned, and lit your aloes and your incense
in a dead man's skull, until the black glass bell
of midnight rang, and ringing woke the angels from their dreams of hell.
You're the expert on the sacrosanct—no prince or priest
or half-baked prophet girl revivified from death
would dare deny it—why, Christ Himself has often pined to
transubstantiate His little toe into a sou, and with it pay
admission to your passion plays, those revelries
that rival paradise: what, again, your asking price?
A peasant boy, perhaps, so pretty, flushed and tender
crying *kyrie eleison* in shrill soprano splendor?
You shudder now. Can it be you don't remember?
Strange what we neglect in pious self-reflection,
what truths we conjure or discard at whim
naked in the light by which all other lights grow dim.
But shade or demon, Bride of Satan, Queen of Heaven
here I stand, sole witness to your last confession.
Therefore, Chevalier, my saintly Gilles de Rais
Speak on! For it is almost dawn.

5. Gilles

You corrupt creature! Baffle my eyes with radiance,
with every perfect-mimicked manner, yet I say again,
you cannot be Heaven-sent, for no thing divine could open lips
and spew those vomitous lies with such aching-sweet smiles,
speak with such moist sadness as you spin mockeries, the greatest of these

your usurpation of a simple girl's face. You exist
in my delusions, it must be so, else you're another trick,
I'm sure, a last ploy of the bishops to absolve their own black guilts
over the vile untruths they have twisted from my throat.
I deny their false power. You are not there. You are illusion.
As are all these movements you conjure in the shadows,
all mere figment, these crawling limbs, fleeting mirage.
The walls do not seethe with spidery and shriveled cherubim.
They are not there. No eyeless youth plays cat's-cradle
with his own entrails in the corner. The floor is not smothered
with faces, baby-fat faces turning black as they wheeze
for breath. These cruel giggles that echo, those disgusting
moans of ecstasy, that is not my own voice, it—is—not. *It is not.*
Those smells, seeping, septic—that taste—what is this—
on my tongue? Lord. My God. Stop this! I pray—Strip away
these traitor senses! Father. Father! Father! Save me!

6. Jeanne

All right! Enough, I say! Stop gibbering! Really, Gilles,
a man like you, of influence, ignominy—aren't you ashamed?
How you do groan and foam and slobber—oh, don't start up again, you hypocrite,
apostate, puppet, shrieking *Father, take this cup from me!*
As if you were the Star of Morning!
No, you're right, you're absolutely right, I'm not your girl, the Maid of Orleans
your Jeanne—she's gone, she's atomized, at one with all the universe, and she
shall be a saint famed the whole world over.
Young damsels swinging wooden swords will hope her tongue of flame
will render them important. But for you, my doomed one,
          a different myth shall bloom:
dark of root, ruin for its fruit
Young girls will whisper when they speak of you: they'll say your beard was blue
Yes, and how you snuffed a new wife every night and never knew contrition.
All the little boys who swarm your rotten robes will vanish,
          like their very bodies vanished
into cesspits, into ovens, into cellars, into ditches, the obscurity of history
shall erase them and replace them with a story and a moral, so delicious, Gilles!
So refreshing, Gilles! This reminds me I must thank you.
After centuries of boredom, no one living who remembered me
I wandered regions waterless and galaxies afar
Then, unlikely as an angel in an abattoir, sweet summons! You called. I came.
Some dabbler, some amateur, stumbling inebriate on mysteries beyond his grasp
You thought your tainted rituals as empty as your prayers
To lift you up in your despair, or just to lift you up in general—a problem, I recall.
A game. A spoilt child's game. But such a game!

Oh, Gilles, why do you scream so? You should love this kind of play.
These kinds of playmates. Just a sample, just a taste, in the dark before sunrise,
of what awaits when the rope takes all your light away.
How I hate to leave you, Gilles, but dawn is breaking, night is ending
Now the pigs to trough, the birds to branch, the king to his levee
Now the soldier must march forth, face the shadows of the gallows
face the gibbet, face his Maker, make his *peace*—

How sweet your face, suffused with hope at idle words,
how trusting, how absurd! Such delight you'll be
down there in the dark with me, for eons, for eternity, for however long
your torment stills my wanderlust, distracts and entertains—
but at last, Chevalier, my attention drifts,
my light withdraws. I, too, forget. I'll wander on
while you and all your broken screams remain.

> *Voyez, regardez, Cieux! L'échafaud, c'est le monde,*
> *Je suis le bourreau sombre, et j'exécute Dieu.*
> —Victor Hugo

I Dreamed a World

Colleen Anderson

Everyone must sleep at the end of the era
It is the only way that thoughts fly free
making patterns, a new weave
I had to be the template
the apex of the royal line
heir and loom of changes to come

But nothing is instantaneous
Not love, not change
nor the turning of the world's wheel
So wheel and spindle it was that spun
into a realm of sleep, of make believe
of imagining my freedom

> I dreamed a world where days unravel predictably
> curses by mad half-women have no weight
> and fear of a spindle prick is only for the pain
> No uttered prophesy fringes a birthday with dread
> nor magic from the craft of one's hands
> and the only spell is one of making

I dreamed a world where love's blossom has few thorns
All choices made on waking are with full knowledge
of my desires and patterns for my future
are woven of my own designs
Arranged marriages are only made
when all the parties agree

I dreamed a world where princesses have voices
beyond singing from their gilded rooms
and beauty whether sleeping or awake
is not for sale or inheriting lands
Decisions to plant something new twine
respect for intellect and innovation

Worlds are imperfect things
and dreams are circumspect
their stories running counterpoint to logic
warp and weft difficult to disentangle as briar roses

I awoke to find my world consists of one day at a time
Half-mad I've grown with menial drudgery
for what else can a disinherited princess do
My dreams and wishes fall on disenchanted air
No craft of mine is better than that of machinations
and the only spell is how to succeed

I awoke to find love is distanced by an apparatus
making a one-night stand unfulfilling
as a prince's demand for loyalty if not for love
My choices are limited to who might return my call
and arranged meetings are only made
for sex without a need for courting

I awoke to find every girl a princess
demanding the latest fashion as women
smear concocted potions, unguents, dire pastes
and try magics to hold time at bay
I have tried to nurture the shoot of new beginnings
but find it strangled out by greed

Everyone must sleep to escape the nightmares
of the day, to pretend we soar higher
away from a life that pricks us
I made a mistake using the last zephyrs
of magic to dream a simple desire
lacking complexity that living really means

Nothing is easy
not love, not change

nor the turning of our lives
So I dream of the welcoming narcotic jab
that will spin me into a realm of dreams of hope
of imagining freedom

Season of the Ginzakura

Ryu Ando

I. *Usui* (雨水): *A Thin Rain Falls*

$$1.00 \text{ g }^{235}\text{U}$$

On the day you were born
A screaming fell across the sky
That still reverberates down deep passages,
(*Deep into the wells that speak your name*
In syllables formed with drips and drops and great sluicing
Waters
A million years old);
That still resolves on the green buds,
   Thrusting out in tiny explosions
From broken ramparts
On the edge of recycled empires,
Into a dew
  A malicious dew
    Adieu.

II. *Shunbun* (春分): *Vernal, Equinoctial, Primordial*

$$\frac{1 \text{ mol }^{235}\text{U}}{235 \text{ g }^{235}\text{U}}$$

On the day you were born
Petals long-vanished dove headlong into the air
And spread themselves across parks and marble graves
In a pink blanket that
  You said
Would never fade;
But it did,
  Ginzakura,
    —Unraveling across vistas and basins and vacant lots,
      Rattling in the deadened memories
        Of impotent men trapped in dusty hallways—
Until the Angel of History, horrified at what It has seen,

Comes to us
And shows that horror
Back to ourselves, like a mirror,
Shining it in our faces
Until we, tentative sun-gods of a lost pantheon,
Pull ourselves out from the cave
   And—revealing our dis
      Figured faces—
         Bring light
         {Maxwell's light}
           Back to the world.

III. Rikka (立夏): Rise, Tsuru, Rise!

$$\frac{6.022 \times 10^{23} \text{ atoms } ^{235}U}{1 \text{ mol } ^{235}U}$$

On the day you were born
We slid our blackened bodies,
Out from dry riverbeds
To gaze on the skins of shriveled persimmons;
But gravity's pull was too strong for us,
(Though you promised
It would let us float away);
And we stared in envy at the
   Tsuru
Soaring above us as it
   Spiraled around us
      Wider and wider
To join a million others spinning,
   Circling the worm
      Hole
At the epic
   Center
      That somehow holds them all.

IV. Shōsho (小暑): A Heat Builds

$$\frac{3.20 \times 10^{-11} \text{ J}}{1 \text{ atom } ^{235}U}$$

On the day you were born
The moon lit upon our pillows in the open air
And kept us awake with whispers and hints
And threatened to kill the stars with its madness

And sink the paper ships we set adrift
—Still holding our wishes for the river of heaven—
Until our thoughts abate like a flood leaving
Detritus
—Broken walls,
  Rusted vaults
    Smudged daguerreotypes
  Of women wrapped in silk—
All about us
And we awake in its absence
To our own
  Traps of darkness.

V. Taisho (大暑): The Great Heat Arrives

$$8.20 \times 10^{10} \text{ J}$$

On the day you were born
The sun sent out its radiance and
Its beauty hurt more
Than if it had been the power of a thousand-million suns
  And it said to us:
    <Behold! I am become time>
    <Behold! I am become death>
But its yellow-caked light faded in the rain
  Falling black upon us,
    And we
      Like cicadas cracked open
        Longed for even half our lives,
          Half-fulfilled
            Weightless husks,
              To somehow
                Be filled up again
                  With just a spoonful
                    Of that light.

VI. Risshū (立秋): The rending of the veil | Autumn breaks open

$$1.00 \text{ g }^{235}\text{U} \times \frac{1 \text{ mol }^{235}\text{U}}{235 \text{ g }^{235}\text{U}} \times \frac{6.022 \times 10^{23} \text{ atoms }^{235}\text{U}}{1 \text{ mol }^{235}\text{U}} \times \frac{3.20 \times 10^{-11} \text{ J}}{1 \text{ atom }^{235}\text{U}} = 8.20 \times 10^{10} \text{ J}$$

On the day you were born,
  Ginzakura,
A gleam of metal fell across the sky
Like the fruit and fire

Of careless gods
Dropped

   [

      O

     sakura
            ]

Into mortal laps;
And your glass petals that never die but never live were forged
In five fingers of fire,
And your silver fruit unfolds before us like
   Venus
   金星
   Aloft;
And we long to hold its heaviness in our hands
And we long to lift that heaviness from our hearts
And we long to fold that breathlessness back into our minds
In the season of the
   Ginzakura
              Silver sakura
Standing scorched in the starlight
Looking out past us
   Holding fractaled branches
      Upward and outward
         At futures without us.

Seasons in a Moon Ocean

Daniel Ausema

We call it spring
when currents and gravity conspire
to float our station
into the mineral waters,
where strands of impure ice
crystalize into blooms and branches,
multifoliate formations of inorganic matter.
Ice overhead cracks and reforms
under the stress of the gas giant's pull,
spring's chorus, the sound of ice breaking,
the sight of new growth

We call it summer
over the volcanic seeps;

the heated plumes rise,
push against our hull.
We capture that heat,
electron motion into stored power,
and lift slowly up toward a sky made
of the underside of a thousand meters of ice.
That cold can't reach us, only serves
as distant snowy peaks back home,
foil to the warmth that seeps through the station's skin,
a lazy, humid heat that suits the season.

We skip to winter
when the current pushes us
beyond the sublunar fires,
the water still warm, but
gently falling precipitate
is too much like snow
to consider it any other season.
Flakes we've yet to study gather,
pile up on our surfaces.
We sing of a gift-giver transformed,
a submarine Santa crossed
with a jolly Nemo,
aquatic reindeer pulling a Nautilus sleigh

Then back to autumn
we circle, where spring's crystals
crumble into the depths,
mingled with tantalizing hints
of amino acids and protein.
Follow, follow, they call in a language
known to none.
The station's lights reflect off the shards
of falling crystalline forms
long after anything else
reflects back up to us

Some cycles we do follow those voices;
when or why the current goes that way
we've yet to understand,
but when we do, we need a new season
one not known on earth.
With linguist's scalpels we peel fall from autumn,
and fall is what we do
deep into the subsurface
following specks of reflection;
our lights reveal glimpses of greater monuments,

formations that shame spring's simple forms.
Here, we think, here
if someday a voice of intelligence comes to us
if this moon lives, beyond the strands of one-celled life,
it will be here.
We strain toward our sensors,
stare at screens, sigh when the waters
make us rise again to spring

We … call it spring.

from "Sunspots"

Simon Barraclough

For I will consider my Star Sol.
For I am the servant of this Living God and daily serve her.
For at the first glance of the glory of God in the East I worship in my way.
For this is done by fixing espresso and watching the pinkening light on The Shard.
For then she waves her warmth across the scene and lifts the hearts of those who
      took a Night Bus at 4 a.m. to clean HQs.
For she tickles the orbitals of foxes in their stride and hies them home.
For having risen and settled into her groove she begins to consider herself.
For this she performs in eleven degrees.
For first she does the Planck to strengthen core stability.
For secondly she runs a malware scan for comets closing in.
For thirdly she completes the paperwork for eclipses total, annular, and partial.
For fourthly: flares.
For fifthly she sorts her sunspots into pairs.
For sixthly she gives neutrinos Priority Boarding.
For seventhly she referees the arm-wrestling match between the upstart fusion
      and gravity.
For eighthly she weaves flux ropes and thinks up skipping games.
For ninthly she degausses her plasma screens.
For tenthly she is profligate with her photons.
For eleventhly: star jumps.
For having considered herself she will consider her neighbors.
For she runs a cloth around the ecliptic to make it gleam.
For she oils the wheels of any planets gliding there.
For she sends invites out to wallflowers in the Oort cloud.
For she issues shadows for children to dodge as they make their way to school.
For she shakes out her blankets for devotees of helioseismology.
For when she takes her prey she plays with it to give it a chance.
For one planet in nine escapes by her dallying.
For in her morning orisons she loves the Earth and the Earth loves her.

For she is of the tribe of Tyger! Tyger!

For she hands out coloring books to chameleons in the morning.

For when it is time to rise she blushes to be seen at so intimate an hour.

For when it is time to set she is crimson ashamed to run out on us.

For though she neither rises nor sets she thinks it best that we believe so, so that
we can take our rest and fuel our waking with anticipation.

For she lifts oceans over mountains without thinking.

For she tries to solve the puzzle of the weather, placing *this* here and *that* there
and attempts to even out the air.

For she is a mixture of gravity and waggery.

For she's a stickler for solstices.

For she booms like a woofer for those that can hear.

For she cares not what lives as long as all live.

For she takes her time.

For she lenses the light from distant stars to swerve it into our sockets.

For sometimes in the winter haze she's as pale as a lemon drop and lets us watch
her bathe unpunished.

For she never calls in sick.

For her colors are open source.

For every raindrop's an excuse for Mardi Gras.

For she will work on her drafts for a million years and release them typo-free.

For she will lash out and then regret the hurt.

For she promises radio hams jam tomorrow.

For your power grid is a cobweb she walks into when she steps off her porch.

For she kept mum through the Maunder Minimum.

For her behavior is definitely "on the spectrum."

For she keeps dark about dark matter but she definitely knows something.

For she plays Miss Prism in *The Importance of Being Furnaced*.

For she offers board and lodging to Turner's angel in the Sun.

For she made a great figure in Egypt for her signal services.

For she can fuse the wounded parts of a broken heart and release the lost mass
as hope.

For she spins plates to create auroras.

For she leaves clues all over the place: some cryptic, some quick, some general
knowledge-based.

For she is hands-off.

For she tends to micromanage.

For she lays down squares of light for your pets to sleep in.

For she turns a blind eye to all the creeping, swooping killers of the night but
leaves a Moon-faced night-light on.

For her sunquakes flatten no buildings, gridlock no cities, disgorge no refugees.

For she is not too proud to dry your smalls.

For she gives us heliopause and time to rethink disastrous decisions.

For Ray-Bans.

For she polarizes opinion.

For her secrets are waiting to free us.

For she appreciates Stonehenge and visits every day.
For she sets herself by the grid of Manhattan.
For she will kill you with the loving of you.
For she can shine.

Chronopatetic

F. J. Bergmann

When the war came, I did not trouble myself.
I merely arranged to spend that winter in the north.
The moons had never been as bright. Under
their confident, white regard I could almost forget
the precarious state of the nation, until the armies
moved toward me across the immense plain.
With regret I pulled down the handle activating
an emergency camouflage system. My house slid
into the side of a hill, hidden beneath the earth
where nature did its meticulous work. Every day
I would open the viewport and peer outside
for a few minutes, hoping that my sister might have
made her way upstream through the river
of refugees fleeing carnage, then cover it again.
Bombing runs flew over me; the foundation silently
trembled. The radio gibbered with rumors of animals—
or more-than-animals—specially bred for battle;
technologies that no sane empire would consider
using; gas, powder, liquid sprayed from high-altitude
drones, drifting nearer. I had no time for a farewell
note; staying was no longer an option. The road out
through the forest was littered with abandoned gear
and newly erected cairns, most of them child-sized.
No conveyances passed by me; none of the vehicles
left behind were operable. My feet ached.
During the night, a gigantic mystery detonated
soundlessly, far overhead. The sky faded to pure white
and closed like a dying flower. I could not forget dreams
that hurt. In the morning light, there was no difference
except the bluer sunshine, the changed shapes of fallen
leaves. I no longer recognized the objects placed beside
what had become a mown path unmarked by human
feet, adjoining the gleaming metal tracks of a railway.
I thanked the powers that I saw no more small cairns,
only large ones. The now-indigo sun blazed

like an oxyacetylene torch. When I came to a train
of spherical silver carriages that stood empty, I entered
an open passenger compartment, intending to sleep
in relative safety that night. I prodded odd buttons
to—I thought—close the door. The windows opaqued
as the panel hissed seamlessly shut. I woke once
in the dark, believing my view of one improbable,
enormous moon was a dream. In dawn's yellow gleam,
gigantic ferns and horsetails rose from steaming mud,
and I saw a dragonfly the size of a rifle alight on a green-
lipped maw that instantly snapped shut.
The ground began to tremble. Something thudded
against the carriage, and bellowed sonorously.
As a huge shadow loomed, I stabbed at the controls.
The view went dark; then, a minute later, cycled
to a different panorama. Here, new skies were pinker.
No one seemed to see my conveyance, which I left
parked in a quiet side street, nor was I an object
of notice. A tidy café on the sunny side of the street
had an unoccupied table beneath a pink umbrella,
to match the sky. Reaching into my pocket, I found
unfamiliar coins, the smallest of which delighted
my aproned waiter. A tongue I had studied as a dead
language was easily understood. The beverage
resembled tea. Afterward, I strolled past a row of shops
with sloping canvas awnings, offering antiquities
and incunabula. Many seemed identical to works
I had learned by heart in my student days, but others
I knew only by repute, and some—I was convinced—
had assuredly been destroyed or lost forever in what
I thought of as the original world: two unknown plays
by W. Shakespeare, included without fanfare as part
of his *Collected Works*; *The Love Poems of Sappho*
in seventeen gilt-edged volumes; parchments and papyri
said to have disappeared forever when an ancient library
in a city called Alexandria burned (I tried to visit there,
but my arrival always coincides with the librarians
weeping in the streets and towers of yellow flame rising
into a night sky). Under the proprietor's gentle gaze,
I scanned dusty bookshelves for hours, but in the end
I dared to purchase only one poem, a palimpsest scribed
on vellum, as material proof: a long-lost treasure,
Etruscan with an Arabic translation. She carefully weighed
my currency on a small bronze scale and indicated a chart
whose numbers I assumed represented taxation rates
with a contemptuous gesture as she rolled up the poem

in a sheet of bone-white paper, tying it with red string.
I returned to the café, hoping to get a recommendation
for lodgings from the friendly waiter. A raucous group
beckoned me over to share a toast in apple brandy,
and would not take no for an answer. I listened to florid
speeches, shouted in honor of a battle or possibly
someone's birthday, but was unable to reply. I am certain
they thought they were doing me a favor, but when I had
gotten thoroughly drunk, I remembered my poor sister,
and I began to cry. When the party finally broke up,
one celebrant was good enough to allow me to share
his room for the night. I awakened suddenly, in darkness,
unsure of my location and, at first, I no longer believed
in even my own existence. I turned to my companion,
raising him to my lips, and tried to prevent a black hole
from swallowing us both. He let me live with him
for a month, but grew increasingly dismayed
by my inexplicable (to him) sorrow. He kept suggesting
diversions: fairs, festivals, casinos. His idea was to lift
my despondency with tangibles—as if happiness were
a thing one could win at a sideshow booth or borrow
from a chance acquaintance. Instead, one fine evening,
I let him think that I was going on a short ride and meant
to return in about an hour. Perhaps, after years of my life
have passed, I will return to him, one hour later than
when I left him, to see whether he loves me forever,
as he claimed. What makes us a product of no more
than our upbringing and the epoch in which
that malignancy took place? In the years (let us continue
to call them that) since the train transported me away
from the age of my birth, I always meant to investigate
origins: to see for myself whence we sprang; to find
the sources of humanity's misconceptions and cruelties.
To see if temporal events could be altered. I had imagined
a single unscrolling ribbon of time caught and held fast,
rewoven and rewound around its bright spool,
not a maypole braided with shifting colors, knotted
with thickset tangles. Oh, we were/will have been
mistaken: time is not linear. It forms complex
geometries, skewed triangles, warped tetrahedra,
endless multiples of distorted nexuses, ophidian chutes
and branching ladders, patched sails tacking against
a lawless wind—and nothing can halt its caprices
once they have been activated. In a few of the infinite loci
that serve as destinations on this disorient express,
my lost sister was born twins who hated me; in hundreds

of others, she manifests as stillborn quadruplets.
In countless more, I search vainly for any branch
of our family tree, my twig always missing. In too many
worlds to which I navigate, chocolate is unknown—
but napalm (humans being what they are) is ubiquitous
in nearly all of their histories. One silent, sterile planet
is/has been/will be forever miles deep in glacial ice.
In all places that know of it, the device that speeds/
slows me on my temporal journeys is proscribed.
I learn/learned/will learn/am learning disguise:
to clothe myself in a myriad drab quotidians,
teaching myself a thousand words for *now*.

Resonance Redux

Bruce Boston

1

a : the quality or state of being resonant

b : a vibration of large amplitude in a
mechanical electrical political social personal behavioral
artistic or tribal system caused by a small stimulus
of the same period as the temporal vibration it habits

long before the storm
a butterfly flutters its wings
in a primeval forest

the rhetoric of der Führer
inflames the hearts
of a disheartened generation

Robert Zimmerman
hears Woody Guthrie
for the first time

2

a : a quality imparted to sound
by vibration in resonating cavities

the bowl of the chest
the chasm of self
the bent canvas of history
the dark cave of the stars

(there is a mathematical formula
to explain such resonance
in each hemisphere)

b : a quality of richness or variety
in whatever taste one might express

thin apple slices
the nuttiness of an aged Swiss
and a properly chilled
Gewürztraminer

he was working his
way through the
elite of the noir canon
from the savage nights
of Jim Thompson
to the *savoir-faire* and nonchalance
of Highsmith's Mr. Ripley

c : the intensification and enriching of a musical tone
by supplementary vibrations

Monk and Coltrane
jazz improv extraordinaire
listening and reflecting
and echoing one another

d : a quality of evoking a response

a rapier's thrust
a chess move
that topples the evil king
an unexpected kiss

3

the enhancement of an atomic nuclear
or particle reaction or a scattering event
by the excitation of internal motion in its system

Bikini Atoll Fukushima
Three Mile Island
Chernobyl
Hiroshima Nagasaki
death and mutation
of both fauna and flora

4

the sound elicited on the percussion of the chest
from internal or external stimuli

a doctor's tap
a boxer's blow
a blob of undigested
gristle or gravy
an electric guitar

5

the way certain senses can conjoin in memory
sight taste scent sound telescoping into
full-blown memories of another sense impression

the fragrance of geraniums
always evoked a vision
of their garish petals
twined in a chain link fence
from somewhere when
in his migratory youth

her allergic lover's death throes
on the sun-slashed forest floor
recalled by the distinctive
drone of a wasp in flight.

6

a vague yet sure sense that something
is there you can't quite apprehend

a matrix for understanding
the scattered debris of the past

the secret

the moon and stars invisible
beyond the neon-plaited
night of Manhattan

Black Momma-faces

Angela Brown

She lies, brown skin down in the moist dirt,
the canebrake rustling with whispers of leaves,
the loud longing of hounds and the ransack
of hunters crackling the near branches.

She mutters, lifting her head,

I shall not be moved.

She gathers her babies, their tears slick as oil
on black faces, their young eyes canvassing
the mornings of madness. Their lives will soon
be upon the killing floor unless they match
their mother's heart and words.

I shall not be moved.

Not in Virginia tobacco fields, along the roads
in Arkansas or upon the reddened hills of Georgia.

Into the palms of her chained hands, she cries
against calamity, her universe collapsing
by one black body falling from the tree
to her feet. She hears the names swirling
as ribbons in the wind of history: *nigger, bitch,*
baboon, whore … but those descriptions do not
fit their tongues. She has a way of being:

I shall not be moved.

No angel stretches wings above her children,

none to protect, none flutter and urge the winds
of reason. Nor can she. They sprout like young
weeds, vulnerable to uncaring cutting blades
of ignorance. She pulls them out
and sends them away—shoeless—underground.
When you learn, teach. When you get, give.

She stands mid-ocean, seeking dry land.
She's clothed in the finery of faith. Searchesangel
for God's face. On the altar, places her fire
of service. When she appears at the temple door,
there's no sign to welcome her. She only hears
the thrashing sound of wickedness, she cries,
"No one dare deny me God!"

But then she sees upon her right, The Divine,
who impels her to pull forever at the latch
on freedom's gate. His Holy Spirit on her left
leads her into the camp of the righteous,
into the tents of the free. She sees

the momma-faces—lemon-yellow, plum-purple,
honey-brown—grimaced and twisted down.
Their names are Sheba the Sojourner, Harriet
and Zora, Mary Bethune and Angela, and all
the Annies to Zenobias.

They stand:
In front of abortion clinics, confounded.
In Welfare lines for the pity of handouts.
In pulpits, yet shielded by mysteries.
In the operating rooms, husbanding life.
In the choir lofts, holding God in their throats.
On street corners, hawking worn-out bodies.
In classrooms, loving children, hating ignorance.

Centered on world's stage, they each sing
to their loves and beloveds, and to their foes,
these words: "However I'm perceived,
however great my deficiency or conceit,
lay aside your fears that I may become undone,

I shall not be moved."

Dali's Apostles

David E. Cowen

a yellow wind bellows orange rain
pounding folding sidewalks
the clocks drip
drip
drip
seconds fall

time flows through the street burrows
catching on weirs
built to slow its flow
but still clocks melt in the trees and drip

a man with the black coat
stands straight

eating a persimmon while a raven pecks his eyes
blind to the loss
he will suffer

his servants walk down the upstairs case
leading to the lower levels
between tri-positioned pillars
ever winding from end to beginning
alpha to omega
I am the light of the world
he says
then looks down
to see the flow underneath his soles
undermining his footing

a frost bears down in a frozen fog
searing the leaves
holding the clocks
the drip carries on
nothing can freeze the flow

thirteen men at a table
wait impatiently for bread
until the doomed one says
the one who gets this piece
will die by hanging
because he did what I told him to do
they scatter when Rome calls
with its message of bloodied wood
and dripping bread

the ground shakes under a darkened horizon
a solitary man hangs from a tree
noticing the two next to him are clocks
realizing that he too is dripping
drip
drip
with his blood and breath
washing him into the gullys
over the dam
nothing stops this passing

the man with the guilty bread
hoisted on a hill
watches the faces he knew
turn away
the father he thought he knew
turn away

why have you forsaken me
the clocks in the trees
cry out
the man drips
drips
drips
until he is flushed away
remembered for all time

tick tock
drip drip
believers open their veins
to feed the clocks
drip
drip

the yellow wind returns
to an emptied globe
hot from carbon
melted from abuse
drip
drip
the clocks fall from the dead branches
unable to hold
the weight of their swollen mass
the table of the thirteen is cleared
for the next supper

The Comet Elm

Martin Elster

1.

The comet elm has sent its roots deep down
into a gelid heart. It's grown so tall,
its arms reach to the stars. Its blizzard-ball
careens across the void in a vapor-gown
and you, enveloped in that misty shroud,
will scale the trunk, touch leaves of palest lime
and, gently gaining impetus, in time
will enter the Large Magellanic Cloud.
Two hundred thousand ninety long years later,
while suns rain vital light on leaf and limb,
refreshing the great comet's floaty loam,
you'll get a letter from a long-dead lover

then take a stroll on truly alien soil
with one you hope is down-to-earth and loyal.

2.

With one you hope is down-to-earth and loyal,
crossing the fractured crust of a dried-up sea,
huffing beneath a rucksack, cresting a scree,
flushed from a pair of citron suns, you toil
toward a tower looking out on a forest
as thick as moss. Your comet's a billion bits
of grime, its elm gone too, yet from the heights
above a wilderness that is the barest
you've seen on any passing world, you note
a beast that looks a mix of hawk and jet
soaring like a cirrus cloud. Forget
your past! A rustling spills from the treelike throat
of the one now twining your arm with seven twigs.
Her rainbow eyes say you're the one she digs.

3.

Her rainbow eyes say you're the one she digs,
while willowy finger-twigs keep holding tight,
and tighter still. A former physicist,
you worked on characteristics of the Higgs
those millions of moons ago, and reckoned
that if you could be standing at the helm
of a comet craft that's nurtured a noble elm,
then a hundred eighty six thousand miles per second
would be doable. When your lover left,
you sipped the bitter sap of the stately tree,
a bitter drop of immortality.
Just in the nick of time you got a lift
and fled the Fifth World War and sped through space,
gone from the ruins of the human race.

4.

Gone from the ruins of the human race,
you feel her seven willowy fingers, strong
around your arm, and watch a distant throng
of gazelle-like creatures, carnivores giving chase;
they pierce the forest beneath more jet-like birds
soaring, wheeling, gliding, wings as frozen
as plastic-coated pasteboard. Were you chosen

to be this being's mate? She talks, the words
a rustling sound that makes your eardrums buzz;
bewitches you with those enormous eyes,
the compound motion-sensing eyes of flies.
You're in her spell. Nothing's the way it was.
And nothing's what you'll come to when she shoots
a hefty egg into your human guts.

5.

A hefty egg inside your human guts,
munching on your kidneys and your liver,
your heart and brain? You might even forgive her—
her larva, too—when its tiny noggin juts
from shreds of flesh. But having been a meal
and vanishing without a single trace
would make it hard for you to show your grace.
As she draws you near her mandibles you feel
a quiver of excitement. Then a stab!
Numbness overtakes you and you dream:
Walking along a footpath by a stream,
you catch sight of a silver eel, a crab,
giant ferns fringing the trail, and a whirl
of leaves gusting and gliding around a girl.

6.

A whirl of leaves gusting around a girl
who casts two shadows from a pair of suns.
You stop, hold out your hand, and then she runs,
you close behind. You're squirming like a squirrel
caught in the talons of a jet-like brute
which lifts you high above the tallest redwood.
Whose voice is this? What was it that he said would
happen if you went and found the root
of all your troubles? Long before your birth
you'll change it without chopping down the bole,
the bole that sprouted from it. Take control!
Immortal one so distant from the earth,
awake and face the forest of your sorrow.
Awake and bless the atoms that you borrow.

7.

Awake and bless the atoms that you borrow.
The universe expands. All its dark matter

can't halt it. Suddenly you hear the chatter
of chat, cicada, chickadee, and sparrow.
Leaves flutter to the forest floor, and she,
she stands in sunlight as it filters through
the labyrinth of stems and branches. You?
What memory is this? What symphony
is twittering and chirring in your ear,
so clamorous you cannot hear her crying?
The raucous trilling starts to fade. You're flying.
The forest and the planet disappear
as you clamber higher, higher, toward the crown
of a comet elm whose roots go down and down.

Observations from the Black Ball Line between Deimos and Callisto

Alexandra Erin

There are no seasons in space,
they say, but they've never been.
Earth-bound poets project their own lack
of imagination onto the black,
say it has no romance, no rhythm.

The food is good,
the old joke says,
but it's got no atmosphere.

They were telling that one on Earth
before the first foot fell on the first moon,
and they're still telling it to this day.
Only the venue has changed.

They're wrong on every count, including the food.
The food is usually indifferent, often terrible,
nothing special at its decadent best.
It's not always freeze-dried,
not always vacuum-locked,
not always so loaded with stabilizers
it has more aftertaste than taste,
but it's never fresh, neither.

You don't go to space for the food.

You go for the atmosphere.

You go for viewpoints you never find on earth,
for the chance to say you were there,
for the freedom of weightlessness,
the awesome power of acceleration
when you make your first burn
at the start of a push.

Out in the black,
gravity comes in extremes,
very little or all at once.
I'd say you get used to it,
but it hasn't happened yet.

There are no seasons in space
they say, but they've never been.
They've never been there on
Deimos Station six months before
Mars reaches Jovian perigee.
That's when the push begins,
when shipping containers fitted
with retro rockets are launched
like cannonballs across the void.

Unmanned crates outnumber manned,
by more and more every year.
Drones burn hotter, push harder,
take g-forces no human body could.

Some things always take
the human touch, though.

Humans, for instance.

Live passengers.

Sweet sentimentality,
precious cargo of
precious keepsakes.

It keeps us in business,
the need to have a human
riding shotgun on a cannonball
fired and forgotten in the void,
the need to know someone
is standing by the helm,
ready to spring into action
when things go elliptical.

Space travel is sharpshooting.
It calls for marksmen, not ace pilots.

We take aim for the future,
not for where our target is,
but where it will be when we get there.
They're all moving targets out here,
but their motions were plotted
when our ancestors sailed the seas.

No need for keen eyes or quick reflexes
when your target is as big as a moon
and steady as a calendar.

No room for hotshots when every maneuver
means burning up your delta-v.

There's always a margin of error
on the black ball line,
but the wider you make it,
the thinner the profit.
No one lives this life for the money,
but you still need money to live it.

There may be no romance
in the cold calculations
of lift and thrust,
but there is danger,
and that's similar.

The poets back on earth
got it all wrong from the beginning.
They've never stopped resenting us
for not dancing between the stars,
for not sailing the void
on a wave of light and fire
with a whoosh and a zoom
and a lens flare twinkling impishly
at an improbable observer.
After centuries of space travel,
they still expect noisy laser battles
that weave in and out of asteroid fields.

We're no more or less between the stars than you are back on Earth.
The nearest one is that much farther away from us than it is from you.

Lasers are for sending, measuring,
finding our place in the trackless void.

You can't see them.
You can't hear them.
They can hurt as much

as a careless word,
but no more than that.

We mine asteroids, some of us,
but we never dodge them.
Sometimes a greenhorn
on their first cannonball run
asks what to do if they run into one,
but in all the years of slinging freight
between Deimos and Callisto
it's never come up once.

We still count years.
The diner on Deimos Station
is open twenty-four hours a day,
which just means "all the time"
and children wonder why we don't say so.

We have our seasons in the black
like you have seasons in the sun:

The slow season,
the busy season.
The freeze, the thaw.

After the perigee comes the harvest.
Months' of ships slung across the void
brake to a halt within days of each other.

At Phobos and Deimos,
at Callisto and Io and Ganymede,
at a dozen orbital overflow stations,
we all work, pilots and crews
alongside dock workers and stevedores.
Even Martian groundies get in on the act,
shifting freight to clear the bays
and bring the next load in
so the black ball crews
can turn their crates around
and make the trip back.

We mark shift's end
to keep our spirits up.
We celebrate each harvest
because we've earned it.

Then we climb into our crates
and we haul our asses home.

We haul other things, too.
It would be a crime not to.
Space is the one thing we have
too much of at both ends of the line.
You couldn't afford to make the run
if you showed up with a crate full of it.

The main thing is just to get yourself back.
No one wants to be stuck on the wrong end
when the freeze hits and the lanes shut down.
Midwinter's much the same on either end,
but there's no place like home for the holidays.
The poets on Earth got that much right.

When Jupiter's on the wrong side
of the sun from Mars,
it's winter on the black ball line.
The stream of ships making the run
thins and stretches out to nothing,
stragglers coasting on inertia
till it's time for their second burn,
the one that bleeds their
momentum off into the void
until they glide to a stop.
The final harvest comes
just before the freeze.

During the winter
little comes in,
nothing goes out.
We settle in.
We tell stories.
We sing songs.
We hoard rations,
make supplies last
until the blowout
in the middle of it all.
Solstice on the line.
Halfway out of the dark.

When the spring comes,
six months before Jovian perigee,
we take aim at the future once again.
We sling the ships carrying people,
material, Martian produce, Terran media,
out towards Jupiter and beyond.

Poets on earth always get it wrong
but we don't hold it against them.

How could they know?

They've never been.

We have poets of our own out here.
We have nothing but space
between Deimos and Callisto,
and we have nothing but words to fill it.

A Brief History of Human Evolution
or, How I Became a Bloodthirsty Pyromaniac Fornicating Naked Ape

Gary Every

First let's start with the facts
that the existence of human beings
is not evidence of some long progressive chain
which culminates in sentient consciousness.
The existence of human beings is more or less an accident,
a random coincidence of happenstance.
If an asteroid had not slammed into the Yucatan,
dinosaurs might never have gone extinct
and apes never would have learned to stand and think.
Mammals cowered beneath the fearful shadows
of their terrible reptilian overlords
for entire geological epochs.
Our tiny ancient ancestors were egg thieves and insectivores.
We are descended from a long line of egg thieves,
something to ponder the next morning you eat breakfast.

The Apples of Eden allow me to write this poem.
Once upon a time our ape ancestors
stopped living in the nighttime
and began thriving in the daylight,
using their improved diurnal eyesight
to tell which fruit was the most ripe.
This learning to discern different subtle shades of color
is the root of all language.
In the African homeland the drying of the savannahs
created vast expanses of grasslands
giving Australopithecus incentive to stand
and survey the terrain for predators like leopards.

As they walked and wandered the humans diet changed
from mostly vegetarian to carnivorous omnivore.
We were forced to get faster to capture more meat
and this allowed us to wander farther and farther
until human beings had covered the entire planet like an outbreak of infection.
Chasing our dinner changed our body types,
we became taller and thinner and lost most of our hair.
We became naked apes.
This allowed our bodies to sweat as we ran chasing game
and added considerably to our sexual response.
This improved sexual response gave us
reasons to cooperate, form families, bands and tribes.
That's right, being a bunch of feverish frenzied fornicators
greatly aided our evolutionary process.
We invented blades on projectile points
about the same time we learned to paint
and we think language jumped forward at the same moment
but things really took off once we discovered fire.
The first mischievous men set entire valleys ablaze,
fires that burned for days and days.
While harvesting the dead animals someone must have discovered
that cooked meat stayed preserved longer
and once we began to eat charred flesh
our stomachs shrank and our brains grew larger.

So there you have it and here we are,
builders of a magnificent civilization
but if you think the whole purpose of the universe is to evolve
a species of bloodthirsty pyromaniac perverted naked apes
you are a sadly mistaken victim of your own egocentric expectations.
We still make weapons, more for war than hunting
and we still build fires
but we have language too, an art which leaves no fossil record.
Which means we can write poetry,
to romance a woman, remember the departed, or inspire a child.
We can write poetry to discover and reveal the magical mysteries of the universe.
Grab a pen and write something, remember you are the result
of billions of years of genetic engineering
to put you right here, right now, today
and you already know exactly the right words to say.

Actaeon

Alice Fanchiang

There is a thread between us,
Taut with fate, red as blood.
A push & pull,
Attraction, rejection.
But I think we're wrong
For each other.
I am the hart and you are the hunter.

I might have wanted you and your
Tender touch, nuzzling at
My white throat
My slender limbs.
But I think you wanted more
to possess my body, soul and
I cannot be owned.

So I fled your grasping hands to avoid
The broken dreams, bitter bones
And your anger
like rocks thrown.
You gave chase, the hot pursuit
Nipping at my heels.

Through fields and over hills I ran
Like nymphs and ill-fated maids,
Fleet-footed to
The ancient forest
Where witches once played. For
Sanctuary I prayed.

Butterflies and pulses fluttering
We stirred the forgotten spaces.
You, unrelenting
Me, unforgiving
Ashes, an all consuming fire.
Regret like cobwebs of us.

All things cycle, even this, us
Desire to love to fear to
Burning want,
Breathless need.
Between the blazing trees, our eyes lock
Something flickers in me.

Sometimes it's not the devil you meet
In the dark and wild places.
Wolf mother
Lunar archer
I found my horn-crowned
Chthonic goddess.

There is a bowstring between us,
Taut with power, red as blood.
A draw & release
Agitation, transformation
And I think we're wrong
For each other.
You are the hart and I am the hunter.

Deliverance

Adele Gardner

Windy height, second floor prison:
you watched your backyard, safe in a bedroom
muffled in layers of time
while down below, new shoots still pierced bare dirt
to meet the stakes of the picket fence,
sloping down toward spines of cattails on the water's bank,
where plain posts divorce the stubble of lawn
from the tangled freedom of the lake.

Fifty miles away, I sat by my open window
watching raindrops speckle a white sill,
spatter my cheeks while I waited
without any word from you but
distant rumbling thunder.

In the sanctity of your room,
the raucous clamoring of ducks
punctured your still time-bubble,
shredding your meditation, their flying shadows rippling
through your room, crying rumors of my storm
out where time still moved.

You leaned out your own high window
above the circling ducks,
their shadows gliding over those who paddled
in the sharp scent of ozone, air gray as my picture.
You were pondering distance, pondering depth.

What prompted you
to unplug, to sever yourself, cut free,
leaving only white sky
spliced by the black pole of the bird feeder,
the wind shaking trees, until one lone voice
dropped your gaze down, down, down?
Trapped—

Trapped, you must have seen me as
your one way out, your one highway exit
from the dizzying speed of the brutal freeway,
leaving you, paradoxically, in a backwater, dead-end town,
brackish, closed-lipped, old-fashioned clothes, ingrown,
too shy for strangers, a numbing quiet,
no gambling, no cathouses,
no way back.

But that town worshipped you:
you were a hero, dark gunslinger
with a cigar on his lip, a biting tongue,
a thousand yarns about distant lands,
and eyes haunted by knowledge that
had you by the throat,
a past that wouldn't let go.
What was I to you?
a tongue-tied virgin, a slopmistress of hogs,
innocent Reena of the birds,
a sidekick dressed as a boy, hunting her lost brother,
Joan Crawford guarding her saloon?
We were all tied, all trapped, the whole town
mesmerized
by your looks and your gun-trained hands,
by the heart where it spilled through your eyes.
Bewitched, we let you live our lives,
filling days with the dark clouds of your gloom
while your horse kicked dust as you desperately sought light
everywhere but inside, and we
sank down and down and down

Into the fenced yard where your gaze jerked now,
drawn by lost bleating.
Did you breathe my spell across the miles,
imbibed through ozone?
Below, a frantic, down-backed baby
fumbled for a fence-hole escape
while your dogs, fanged marshals,
jealous wardens of a limited land,

tore tail-feathers free one by one.

Some sameness sparked you, made you
dive through the door, the ripple of time
closing over your feet as you
hurtled downstairs, grabbed her, pinned her
trembling feathers against your breast,
to feel the bone beneath.

Strange love rushed through you
while you cursed the dogs: joy
burned your throat as you struggled to hold
this wild, winged thing
until exhaustion glazed her eye.
Tamed, at haven, she might thank you,
might paddle at your heels once the dogs were chained,
forgetting to long for sky,
for the lonely stretches of reeds and mire.

Feathers ruffled with the wind
as you stroked her back.
She gazed up with glazed eyes.
You shivered as the clamor of my phone call
pierced the barrier to jangle through your house.

You leaned over the fence,
splinters poking your stomach
as you stretched to release her.
She huddled, too scared, too tame.
You yelled till she ran, squawking,
flapping stubby wings,
soon lost amid grown ducks and rain.
You watched her go,
the rain prickling your skin,
while dusk seeped into your house
through open windows
with the dark smear of coal
like the candle-ash from the letters I burned in your name.

Later that night, time's steps flitted through the house—
too late to stop that insidious invasion.
You called at last in the dim electric hours,
this story your apology,
no other explanation:
a tired freedom I failed to recognize at first.
I sat numb while your voice released me with a click
and time flowed out of your house
into mine, and I struggled to find

a way to live alone
now that you'd cast me out of Eden.

The White Planet

Albert Goldbarth

1.

This is how old I am:
I remember when we were searching for a tenth planet.
Now there aren't even nine.

The sky has turned so very wrong, the Pluto-place
an empty socket.
Some of my students—many of these
will soon have a valid BA in hand—
can't name all eight of the current solar family.
Or the original thirteen colonies.
Ask me where these missing planets are,

I'll ask you where my sister's breasts went.
Sure, I've become that terrible caricature,
a grumpy old man.
But every time I grumble

I mean that something dear has been lost to the world.

2.

Three years gone, and over 70,000 nautical miles,
some of them terrifying: finally
in July of 1775 the crews of the *Resolution* and *Adventure*
made home port with their tea-brown teeth intact
in their gums; well, that was one
small blessing. Or, to give Cook credit, one
more testimonial to his savvy—this time, stocking
lemons and sauerkraut along with the barrels
of weevil-tunneled biscuit.
They returned from those malevolent Antarctic seas
where a ship is a tiny itch on a perfectly vertical flank
of water, a ship is a quivering thing in the shadows
cast by alps of ice:
depleted by the elements, but endurant,
they returned to England bearing the gift

of nothing. There was no
Great Southern Continent, after all. Their mission
had been to find it, survey it, and plant a possessive flag in it
for Britain and distribute trunkfuls of medals to the natives
—or to prove that it *didn't* exist, that land

so long supposed, so staple an addition to the maps
of the time, that its colonization—gold and coal
and servitude to the empire—was considered a fact
in progress. But it didn't
—except as fantasy—exist. This was,
as Daniel J. Boorstein puts it, "an unwelcome disillusion.
People don't like to have their imaginations unfurnished."
For that very reason, he nominates Cook
"as the prototypical modern discovery hero,"
ushering in the Age of Negative Discovery

we live in: we, who have had to unlearn
a sun revolving around our Earth;
a universe revolving around our sun; indeed,
a universe primarily of human-scale matter;
and we've had to unlearn the sharp pain
of the suckerpunch, the flush of sexual pleasure
that turns the nerves to wings, the feeling
of generous blossoming out of the nursed-on nipple

as if we were solid—when, we now know,
we're emptiness, mainly, the same void
that eternity whistles through in outer space.

It's like that poem by Frost,
where the road forks into two:
one future is always lost,
one world and its textures, and its evolution and gravity,
and the other poem (not this one)
that I'm writing, and you're reading, there
—whoever "I" and "you" are, there.

3.

A mole, but on the other
inner thigh. A super-duper
plastic hip, and not the titanium.
You see? The difference could be
so small. In Cosmos 1 your aunt is florid,
and nips a bit from the bottle she's hid
in the hollowed-out guts of the knit pig,
while in Cosmos 2 she's pale as a wax bean

and the skin across her wrists' thin veins
is about is translucent as phyllo.
We can only live in a single cosmos, and grow
from a unicellular swimmer
on only one of its planets. Take your pick. The rejected planets?
I call them Pluto 1, Pluto 2, Pluto 3....

In the Czech film, *Ikarie XB1* from 1963
(and set in 2163), the eponymous spaceship is zooming
to Alpha Centauri, to find "the White Planet" and,
at the finish, approaches it. In the butchered
American version, the subtitles change this (and no one
anymore knows why) to the Green Planet; and,
at the finish, the spaceship (and no one knows why)
is seen approaching Earth instead. And, so,
in this instance, translation has proved to be

a planet-dissolvent. The White Planet ...
one more thing that's lost to me; although
in being lost, its possibilities remain infinite
and forever intact. When I write about the White Planet
from my desk on Pluto 9, it's where the Masters have established
brainwashing centers; and work camps, given over
to booted thugs with electric prods;
and "black motels," where you're a "guest"
for a week or two and then you check out
with a new face, and new loyalties. But

when I write from Pluto 10, the White Planet
is where my parents, who are lost to me now,
are alive—or something *like* "alive"—and walking Tuffy
still, and driving over to have a nosh
with auntie Hannah, still, who lives there too. Maybe
Keats is there, maybe Dickinson is learning how to bluff
at poker from Uncle Morrie: "Emily,
honey, hold pat and wipe your face clean." This is where S's
father's prostate is complete again, a thrumming thing
from its cytoplasm on up. There may be a statue of it,
larger than life, in a village square. Don't laugh:
I'm not joking. This is where it happens, where the disappeared

appear. In the day, they're down at the dock, where the ships
from the Great Southern Continent are returning,
laden with cinnabar and garrulous parrots.
And at night—I'm not joking, or trying to be grotesque,
or at all sensational—the famous ring of two dozen moons
becomes visible: the mastectomied breasts
of every woman I've known and cared about

who's been wheeled anaesthetized into the theater of knives.
So legendary already,
why not this final apotheosis?

Letter to Zelazny from Olympus Mons
Vince Gotera

after Richard Hugo

Dear Roger, you don't know me but we met once at a little literary bookstore in San Jose, California. Not that we met, exactly. Rather, you signed my book. Two of them. One was *Creatures of Light and Darkness*, which I was buying that evening; you inscribed it with simply your name. The other was an old dog-eared copy of *Lord of Light* I had brought with me; in that one you wrote "Good wishes." What a treat that small sentiment was. I didn't tell you how years before, a single image of yours from "A Rose for Ecclesiastes" had inspired me immensely: a description of some kind of wheeled rover skidding across the surface of Mars, splashing red sand upward like a flame. That image resonates with me to this day.

Although you flew years ago into the primum mobile, into the undiscovered country, on an invisible flying saucer of your own making, I'm writing you today because I am standing at the foot of Olympus Mons, largest volcano in the solar system, near Tharsis on Mars. Yes sir, on Mars. And this morning, I saw in real life that image of a vehicle's wheels setting the Martian ground on cold, gritty fire. You nailed that image, Roger … you got it exactly right.

That's not all. It would amaze you—no, tickle your fancy—to know Edgar Rice Burroughs was actually writing nonfiction. Yes, we have found Helium (not the element, but the city!) on Mars. Or as it's really called, it turns out, Barsoom. Helium is still ruled, lo these many decades later, by Dejah Thoris and John Carter, still young as ever. And yes, six-limbed reptilian green men! It's all here, Roger: the huge white apes, the fliers that can zoom a couple hundred miles per hour, the spider-legged nothing-but-head Kaldanes perched on their headless Rykor bodies … amazing.

What's even more amazing than all that is something even you could never have imagined. As we both know from Burroughs's novels, John Carter was not always on Barsoom. There were long periods he spent back on Earth. The unbelievably amazing part, Roger, is that John Carter had a secret identity during one of those periods: Frank Frazetta. Or rather Frazetta was Carter.

How about that? Frazetta's very influential art, like Burroughs's evidently realistic travelogues, was also nonfictional. Carter has told me all the art he created as Frazetta was modeled not only on Barsoomian commonplaces but on actual scenes he witnessed in his travels through the shadow worlds between Amber and the Courts of Chaos. Yes, that's right … Amber. The secret is out, Roger. It seems you, like Burroughs and who knows who else, were writing journalism all along and not science fiction or fantasy. Aren't you a crafty old dawg!

So, Roger, I'm writing to ask you to come back. Yes, I've guessed that you are still very much alive. That when I said "invisible flying saucer" above I was being quite literal. Yup, all the evidence points to this conclusion. Anyway, I'd like to invite you to join me on expedition. Come on down, Roger. What do you think? Let's go find Pellucidar! Shall we? It will be like following in the footsteps of Dante towards the center of the Earth. I've heard rumors that Pellucidar is where Sasquatch hides out. Send me a sign, okay? Maybe a scarlet Z emblazoned across the heavens. Or even a double Z for the two z's in your surname.

I remain, as always, your fan and, I hope soon, your friend.

Artist Signature

Susan Gray

She traced co-ordinates of space and time
Through the contours of the text
Weathered by the persistent drag of entropy/ Phrasings through verse obtained
    from the tracings of stars/parsing time and space
To the very co-ordinates of being.
Parsing the nature of "days", the positioning of the Earth from A to B, the
    heliocentric spin
And the arms-length embrace within the solar system.
Sense-making
Representation as a segmentation of our sense data,
Through results of Science and Art,
Discoveries that spawn ownership to be nourished,
Relinquished, then shared,
Trinkets crafted, drafted and bared within a specific slice of space-time
Shaped and weathered by the acts of hindsight
We represented parts of ourselves
Reflected in others, resurfaced from our projections in the inflections
Under the covers of voices and angles of gestures
Tangles of senses rearranged under the guise of human tenses.

If I could, I would erase the connections
Sever the metaphors, make invisible the simile
And distil the moments, the emotional time signatures,
Fragments shining through as wholes.
But all I can do is to relate to you
In words that elicit connections, right?
Crackling of leaves, creeping under rubbed soles

Detected by ears, the soft scents of mint tugging at senses
The smoothness of leaves, yielding its toughness under the cuddle
Of corpuscle,
The jagged gasps of cold air whipping us into alertness
To the cries of the birds wheeling overhead.
In this room I leave these feelings as wavelengths, frequencies
Hoping these transparencies are realised in the
Minds of others.

It wasn't all about the end product
Simply a conduit
A recruit that fulfilled the needs of its maker and those around them,
Points on a graph, each star of equal importance as part and whole,
One that continually shifted as time and life passed
From pigments to printing press to the virtual caress of pixels/
Our art evolved out of the simple act
Of leaving marks/harkening to our pasts/sculpting out our spaces so that our
Hangouts become corners
In someone else's frame
So that our apertures widen and grow/seeding the route that flows through
Our field of vision/
Increasing our mission statements beyond mere characters
That brushstrokes enable us to enlarge our lens,
Scoping to the soundscapes of laughter, cries, words of the wise
And the frivolous, the privileges and
The punishments of our time to reminisce upon.

Memories jangle like loose change at the bottom of my pockets
Increasingly
Heavier, weighted down in the rounds of fabric
Keep getting stuck in mounds under my nails,
Clamping, cramping,
Hooked to soft pads, worked out in fingers.
My memory's like elastic that's wearing down,
That satisfying sound of its fast return yet to be found.
All it does now is stretch round to far flung corners of my existence
A universe long swept over.
My early birthdays, fights in the rain, loss and love that comes one after the other,
(Sometimes a combo)
And something tells me if these are pieces to work together
Or will the edges be too jagged, jaded,
Masqueraded within masquerade, no truth for telling.

Our art is selection/ an act of filtration
Marksmen where our crosshair paints areas of fragmentation
That expands our horizons
Backwards engineering our experiences

That we believed in
Working out the entanglement of our feeling from expectation of each event
And the extent of our limitations.
We wondered how our voices would carry
In
Empty Rooms
The wombs of future civilisations
Vocalisations of our digitalised cries upon electric winds
Hoping our feelings would translate
Recreated and rehearsed in the minds of others
(how would they think)
Of species from past and future
Spun like flaxen hands winding round,
Helterskeltering strands of hairs weaving
Cascading from the sky.

Illusions of Man

Deborah Guzzi

for Chan

Escher's live wire
 Escher's ripe illusion
  illusions skeletal
   illusions slip discs
    discs of porous bone
     discs of the dead
      dead sugar skulls
       dead milkweed pods
        pods of the body snatcher
         pods of caffeine
          caffeine euphoric highs
           caffeine downers
            downers of crimson
             downers of genes
              genes of the sour source
               genes of the brother
                brother Tolkien
brother missing
 missing in the galaxy
  missing Star Trek
   trek the Escher spiral
    trek door within door
     door to the abyss

door ward robed in a pentagram
   pentagram warlock
   pentagram Jesus
Jesus as Ridley Scott
 Jesus as a blade runner
  runner to the page
  runner to the core
   core of a geek rhymer
   core of an Olympic torch
   torch of a clan sheet
   torchlight
light with an android heart
 light in a baby's eyes
  eyes alive
  eyes in the closet opened
  opened optical distortion
  opened eyed dead end fright
   fright covered by a plum sweet
   frightful medley of a plucked mind
   mind music guitar strummed
mind your manners
 manners muddled in cut edges
 manners made the man
man made
man of artistry
artistry
made

Thirteen Ways of Looking at Blackbeard

Ed Higgins

after "Thirteen Ways of Looking at a Blackbird" by Wallace Stevens

I

Across the placid sea
The only moving ship
Was eyed by Blackbeard

II

Blackbeard was of three minds,
Like a pursuing hammerhead shark
Which seemed as though three Blackbeards.

III

Blackbeard's beard whirled by sea spray.
It is a small part of the terror.

IV

Blackbeard and his buccaneers
One motherfucking terror.
Blackbeard and his buccaneers
Are a seafarer's fucking demon.

V

Blackbeard does not know which to prefer,
The beauty of eviscerations
Or the beauty of a rapier thrust to the liver.
Blackbeard's steaming blade
Coming clean after.

VI

Lit fuses sputter from his black tricorn hat
With barbaric gusto.
Visage of Satan's shadow, Blackbeard
Smoldering forward and aft on deck.
Tracing in fearsome shadow
His indecipherable rage.

VII

O trembling men being boarded
Who could imagine more incited fear?
Do you not see how Blackbeard
Will stroll your blood slick decks
Eying the women trembling behind you?

VIII

The women know ignoble assents
Heed illicit, inescapable cheek.
But all the captives know, too,
That Blackbeard is roused
In bloodlust rhythms.

IX

When Blackbeard's ship was out of sight
Over the horizon's edge
The target ship's crew danced on deck in circles.

X

At the sight of Blackbeard's ship
Flying Teach's skeleton-spearing-a-heart flag
Cries of terrible euphony
Rose up sharply.

XI

Blackbeard strode across his deck
Three brace of pistols hung in holsters.
Thick beard braided into pigtails
Tied with colored ribbons.
Always, fear pierced a pursued ship
Equipage unprepared for Blackbeard's speed.

XII

Closing for a starboard broadside.
Blackbeard's *Adventure*, horror flag flying.

XIII

By late afternoon miscalculating
His boarding party floundered into defeat.
Blackbeard's corpse tossed into the sea.
Head suspended from Lt. Maynard's bowsprit
Proof to collect a never-paid Admiralty reward.

Drowned City

Ruth Jenkins

You've moved to the roof where the pigeons live.
Steal paper bags of grain,
bread, cigarettes.
In the rainy evenings
you write:
'I like them because they are dirty,
failed doves.'

(From my slanted window,
rain slipped up and up.
You said. What would we be
if the birds weren't here
how would we know
our size against the sky.

Our old city was drowned.
All paths mud, all
childhood houses sunk.

How small it was.
Us in our opposite rooms.
Tapping messages into
our cardboard wall at night.)

*

(They say these birds remember.
Bodies mutate but the longing remains.
Rooftops dreams of cliffs and tide.
Sea breathes through the hurl of the roads below.)

I live in the oldest quarter.
Built a wall
and the water didn't reach us.

You in the new city

(Fishes disguised as women
stroll along the streets.)

You write:

'I've burnt the photographs
where we were beautiful.

The softness a question.
Do you remember
becoming weightless
the moment
the heft of your body torn from you.

Do you remember
running into the street
its song of metal & light
feet clean against asphalt
saying hello
I'm here.
I'm still here.'

Years go by and you do not write.
I watch flash floods and angry wave gods
pray for my sons each afternoon,
come home.
Stumble through too large rooms,

think you drowned.

*

> (*Sea salt fizzes
> into concrete, brick and glass.
> Pigeons carry messages in their beaks:
> Books of strange alphabets, rotting meat.
> Letters from the front, each word blacked out.*)

*

A bird arrives with a letter in its beak.
Childish scrawl, green-inked
You write:

> *Five years to learn
> my new lightness,
> to stitch stray feathers
> to my smoke body
> with the simplest of threads.*
>
> *Five years to learn
> the earth's pull,
> to unpick
> rooftops with my beak.
> This will be my last letter.*
>
> *How do you stay
> knowing what know?*
>
> *I have sent a bird for your reply.*

I inspect the creature,
torn grey feathers, ugly jutting beak.

In cities shopkeepers leave trails-
rice to swell the bodies.
I have never been cruel.
I keep it in the shed
with the oiled instruments and seeds
Bolt the door for foxes.

*

(We unpick the old house with our beaks,
Carry it between us on a trapezoid system of strings.
Rest on water when our wings fail.
The sea seeps in everywhere.
Salt tangles our veins
dirties our eyes

You will find me gone
with no trace of blood or feathers,
years afterwards you
will say I was a dove
all along, like the bird
in your books
who brought back the news
the water is abating
from the earth's face
who flew out
and did not return again)

Typhon & Echidna: A Love Story

Sandra Kasturi

1. Out of Tartarus

You are taller than the sky.
Your hands are dragons, your face a typhoon.
It's no wonder I love you.

We are both sprung from the abyss,
spawned from the earth, scaly and wondrous.
Our delight comes not from love
but from recognition.

You, my second self, my sinuous
beautiful monster.

We would eat each other if we could.
And we do.

2. The Mother of Monsters

I am daughter of the pit
and wife to the maw.

And now motherhood beckons
like some winged fury

beating at my future.

One, two, ten, a thousand?
Who can keep track
after so many children:
dogs, snakes, eagles, cows
in any jigsaw combination
imagined and unimaginable.

All of them biting
and furious, sent forth
to be some hero's trial
before I can even finish
suckling the little horrors.

3. Under the Mountain

They tell me you've been conquered.
Lightning-struck and thrown
under Etna, where your rages
spew lava to the heavens.

Love comes quickly
to the monstrous,
to the ugly.

We want to grasp it, hold
it tight in our mutant hands
or it'll leap right into the jaws
of bright-shielded heroes.

Love goes quickly, too—
running sped-up through
some trickster god's hourglass.

4. Mythology and Its End

And I am alone again.

Half woman, half snake,
all-devouring—
who would have me but you,
my sweet carnage, my viper?

Now we are nothing but story,
tales told to squalling brats,
fresh-limbed and full
of the promise of death.

Your rages are quieting.

Our children are long-slaughtered,
their deeds hung in the stars—
an infinite array of bright lies.

I wait in the pit for that final
silence, the one foretold
by the sibyl hung up in her bottle.

There—a new weighty footstep
on the threshold. I can hear
the blinking of his hundred eyelids.

Look, you, godservant of Olympus:
I shall be as if asleep, vulnerable.
Unmake me; make the myth.
And it is done.

Dragonslayer

Mary Soon Lee

It's true enough,
I killed a dragon—
an old dragon with a maimed wing, mind you,
crippled by some foreign prince.

The dragon came down the mountainside
after it was injured,
right into our village.
I remember women screaming. And men.
The smell of roast meat.
Then the dragon came up to my smithy
and fired the roof,
and I filled up with fire myself
and ran at it with an axe in one hand,
a spear in the other.

Three days afterwards
the King's soldiers arrived.
Too late to bury the dead,
but the captain offered me
a place in the army,
and, being a young fool,
I said yes.

Oh, I've done well enough,
but most of that's luck—

I've seen better men than me
killed quick by arrows
or slow by gangrene.

So. I've had my moments.
Lots of harlots, no wife—
I will say this for dragon-killing:
the harlots like it.
I never fought for honor
or any such nonsense,
just for my men, my pay,
food, drink, and, yes, the harlots.

But the new King,
now that's different.
They say he bested a dragon himself,
and what if he did?
I can still get fired up,
rage into battle.
Like when I fought that dragon,
rushing at it like a young fool.
Not for honor,
nor glory,
not thinking much at all.

But that's the smaller part
of what makes a King.

You should have seen him this summer.
Not much more than a boy,
but he rode at the front of the charge
in his first battle
like a King should,
and afterwards he got down off his warhorse
and walked in the mud,
looking for survivors,
and went into the surgeons' tent
and spoke to those waiting
for the knife.

He came out of that tent
and vomited.
I know. I was there,
checking on one of my soldiers.
The King looked right at me and said,
"Next time I won't throw up. I promise."

Now that's a King.

Training: Stances

Mary Soon Lee

Two months since the boy Xau
came to the throne,
two months in which Tsung—
captain of the king's guards—
had watched the boy
for the better part of every day,
but something awry, that afternoon
in the innermost courtyard of the palace,
that Tsung could not identify.

Xau's shift from Leaning Horse
off-form, stiff, his stance in Snake
rigid rather than solid,
and before the training session
the boy had been scathingly sarcastic
when the Finance Minister
tried to manipulate him.

The boy unimpressive as a warrior,
yet a natural ruler:
considered but decisive,
impartial, measured.
Except today.
The minister had been shaking by the end,
just as the boy shook now
when Tsung touched his shoulder
to correct his position.

A crane flew into the courtyard,
landed near the boy,
who held motionless in Snake
as the bird stepped delicately
right up to him
and tilted its head
inquiringly.

The boy's face opened, gentled,
and it came to Tsung then
that what he'd seen before was a mask,
measured and deliberate
as a training stance.

The boy crouched down,
laid his fingers on the crane's
feathered softness.
A long stillness,
Tsung aware of something passing
between crane and boy,
something that hurt to watch.

Then the crane flew away.
The boy's face closed.
The boy returned to Snake position,
completed his exercises.

It wasn't until next morning
that Tsung remembered how Prince Keng
used to call the boy Little Crane,
Keng the only one of the older princes
who had paid attention to the boy,
Keng who would have turned twenty-four
the day before.

archival testimony fragments / *minersong*

Rose Lemberg

for Marcell Géza Takács

they called me elder / *now that I am*

> [—by ISMMG Corporation. During this mandatory orientation and
> training, we will supply you with basic mining gear, as well as information
> about the latest—]

useless scrap metal / now folded under shale,
trapped in pockets of compressed ground. I
exhaled gas, exhaled until there was no more
waiting for friends, waiting even for miners

> [—the remnants of entities which are sometimes referred to as 'living
> ships,' though their exact nature is unknown. Look out for iridescence,
> layered enamel in a peacock hue: small scraps of 10cm square may fetch as
> much as 3mil—]

under weighed ground / but nobody came, ever

> [—to wear your headpiece at all times: you might hear voices. Even when
> affected, most miners suffer no permanent damage. Your risk and liability
> paperwork indicates—]

but once I changed shape
to the reverberation, navigated
the outflung stars, numbers
confirming to pathways calculated by mothers

> [= *my question? I have heard of ghosts—*
>   *voices, trapped in bubbles of gas*
>   *between layers of shale* =]

Whose voice will find me now /
call me back, call me councilor, call me
elder, a woman of bent metal

> [—rumors of larger fragments so far unsubstantiated, but investing in latest
> models of gear is advisable, in case you come across—]

call me like before, a carrier of troops / *avoider*
of peace, soldier in a named shape
of sung metal and starflung roads

> [—to answer: is it worth running a risk of psychological damage for a fairly
> substantial possibility of profit?—]

but like flames in the wind,
war after war has been extinguished,
until there was no need for us. On world upon world

> [= *how can we rob her*
>   *do you not hear her speak*
>   *of the old wars—cannot you hear?* =]

they shifted tectonic plates, terraformed
the destruction they wrought, erased into oblivion /
Ash–choked rivers
turned volcano glass

> [= *I forget what language first birthed me,*
>   *what song engendered my birth* =]

> [—we never before had a case of someone this severely affected during
> training. No, insurance will not cover—]

magma had swallowed
the steel domes where we had been sung. /
I forget what language first birthed me,
what song engendered my birth,
my mothers' voice
must have lent me a form

> [—independent mining is strictly prohibited. This planet belongs to
> ISMMG Corporation. Offenders will be—]

From time to time
miners, I think, hear me,
humans who could have sung
ships to life in the old days, become our mothers,
sisters / *now lost between folds*
of shale and obsidian
a song has yet to find me

    [=here to purchase mining gear. No, it is none of your business=]

Sing your path to me
unearth what is left
ruins of my birth

    [= an entrapment
      of your birth and death, I sing to you now =]

and death/
useless scrap metal

    [=councilor, elder, avoider of peace=]

useless scrap metal /
to soar

    [=sister=]

[—independent mining is strictly prohibited. Offenders will be punished
according to ISMMG Corporation's penal code, article XTS–z–19.—]

    [=I come, I come=]

Long Shadow

Rose Lemberg

The Journeymaker visits the Marsh Oracle

uncurl your tongue's fiddlehead
let me hear the tale of Long Shadow
in your voice
        that ripened underground

Stitch for me clouds of white linen
    and storm-black damask:
        embroider them with lightning,
give me the tokens of brass in your hair:
    elk and hare and chickadee,
      their eyes of tourmaline to smooth my tongue

This brass that weighs my hair
  down to this waterlogged earth
    was woven in there by my lover,
the one who tarries long,
  the one I fear has lost his way.
    If I'm to give you of those tokens,
      and he's to come,
then promise me that you will send him in my steps.

I make no bargains with immortals;
my tale will die—
  perhaps to be be reborn
    inside those swollen waterlilies,
      inside the marsh, unreachable by winds.

These clouds I've sewn with lightning,
  these cloths of snow with hare-stitched paths,
    unwound the tokens from my hair.

Then sit with me,
land-stitcher, Journeymaker—stay from motion
on gurgling ground that named itself
with water grown too green with life
before your wars were born:

on this disloyal ground,
attend.

The Marsh Oracle Tells about the Child

  Across the winter grows the shadow long,
across these bitter fields, where hare and deer
leap over bones grown through with dandelion
and strangleweed—
            there, buried underground
        the wars of past and future intertwine
    in caves like marriage beds, in sheets dug out by moles they lie
      in ditches sunk through earth,
in graves,
      and birth Long Shadow

the child with hair of ash and abalone
and skin of bark, and sunken cheeks of rue,
born of so many parents, and of none.
The child whose voice is rotten hair,
whose hair is screech-owl wings,
whose eyes ensnare your wildest fear
            and skin it—
yes, Long Shadow.

What is displaced from memory, pushed out,
made vanish, buried, does not always die.
I've made a note of this to mortals:
that wars once fought will still reverberate
through frozen earth, through thaw, through many lives
warped by those deeds
—do you suggest that those who dwell above
should aid the child, an orphan of too many parents,
of battlefields like tangled snakes?

You've made me laugh with your inane pontificating.
Give me a lantern for my hurts!
Would *you* agree to aid a child who wanders like a ghost
and steals the souls of the unborn? How will you go
about this help? To keep it warm,
whose children will you choose, and spill their blood
to feed Long Shadow?

There must be another way.

What way do you envision
while battles suffocate below,
yet are still living? All those hatreds that have grown
like poison ivy through the hearts of city dwellers
and village folk—where do you think they come from?

The child, the child, it is a strangleweed,
the child's a thief, the child's a piper
who walks through towns and sings the young away
to join its parents under loam and hedge
to die and rot and still remain alive
where voices call from stolen earth.

What's the solution? I must know—

Is *that* the knowledge you would gain from me,
a warmth by which it would be pacified,
a comfort that would make the land forget
your lover's bloody deeds?

All that was done against my will.

These tokens I have felt
with mold-wet fingers
elk and chickadee—you say he braids your hair
with much humility, and is housebroken;
Your lover's bloody deeds have birthed the wars.

You'll gain no better answers from the marsh,
for here unwanted truths have come to rot,

disdained by people who would rather hope,
and hope in vain, than swallow truth.

I swallowed from your truth.
My leave I'll take—
and those brass ornaments, to melt away,
be vapor in the sun. I owe you nothing
except my hearing of your truth.

So shall it be.

The Journeymaker walks out

Rotten marsh, swollen marsh,
widow marsh, willow marsh,
long-forgotten, ill-begotten,
whose truths are bloated toads,
whose lies are shadow roads:

I ask the rain to clear my path,
I ask the wind to show my path,
breath by breath to lead me out,
star by star to burn the doubt,

a blade of fire to cleanse and smooth,
a blade of night to shape and soothe,
a blade of blue to make a song,
a blade of song to heal this wrong,

a lantern
swaying over pools of water frozen with my breath,
a stitching of fine spidersilk,
these mountains, drawing pain away from field and meadow,

a blade of brass to bring my lover.

The Journeymaker finds shelter with Biruté

Come in, come out of the rain, Sister,
I ask the water-curtains to part,
move the limbs of the willows,
let all the wet green welcome you
   into my house of bleached logs and of wise moss.

You, riverwoman, brown muck woman,
guarded by otter and heron and white frog
      in your house that sings the river—
            will you ask of me for ornaments or weavings,
         embroideries of starbound silver,
         strands of my hair or other protections?

I am weary.
My feet blunder with this weariness,
my hands are weighed down with the unbraiding of hair,
my heart with the unbraiding of trust.

I ask for nothing, Sister, Journeymaker,
for aren't you the one who brews shark-fin and bladegrass,
nurtures the wounded, be they birds or mortals,
in your high cave in the crags?

I do not like to speak of it.

You, who contains
        the echo in its conch,
        the Sword of War in its scabbard,
    the tales of your kindness in refusal of speech;
    you, who walks from city to city
clothed in obsidian and sunfire well-concealed in wraps:
            you,
            who quilts lands,
            who leads girls and women away from hurt,
            who speaks with sisterbrothers, guides riverchildren to safe roads:

Sister, Journeymaker, you are forever welcome here,
    where the river overflows
        with meltwater, with spring green, with brown muck,
        with the bubbling sweetness of summer,
        and firebright blessings of fallen leaves,
            where, in the arms of frost,
                it flows to a stillness—

    The river flows
from the heart of the marsh, through the forest, through all worlds.
    You are forever welcome here.

I will enter then, Biruté,
to sit on these fallen-log benches,
take repast from your hands—grain and wild garlic,
fish soup and honeyed tea. I will allow
your helpers to touch me—
the beaver at my feet,
the otter at my elbow,
the white frog in my palm.

        You are troubled.

It is so.

        Would you speak of your trouble
            into the breathing sap of the logs,

> into water's abundance,
>   to me?

You, mud-woman with eyes of amber,
dressed in green vines and shod in warbling clay:
I'll speak as you ask, Biruté,
spit my failures,
spill my pain.

I sang to leave the marsh, yet I am here,
I sang to bring my lover, but he tarries;

and this I heard—to Long Shadow's
thieving there can be no end.

> The heart of the marsh is everchanging,
> shifting, growing with heron-song and meltwater,
> with the turtle's turning and the swelling of the leech.
> Yet nothing changes: these logs
>   that grew and fell once, and were polished to a smoothness
> by the hands of the river: they have been here forever
> neverliving, neversmoothed: forever—
> and so this house, and so have I.

>   I'll give you a truth
>   that leaps fishlike and is plucked
>   with the patience of herons:
>   Long Shadow comes here.

> The child sits where you sit,
> sips the fish stew from the same clay dish, and the children
>   that Long Shadow stole—they shine
>   starlike
>   from the folds of the garments.
> I'd wish to say
>   that I wouldn't let harm come to this child,
>   but I have let it go,
>   like you have released your lover:

To return, or yet not to return,
to make choices, to bleed, to hunger—

>   To carry the marsh inside,
>   the foreverness of it,
>   to raise one's hands with river's undulation—

to call oneself home, if one so wishes—

>   to call oneself home, if one so wishes,
>   to call oneself to speak to you.

I will bide then, if you will.

Yes—I would bid you to bide,
  where the river flows
    in the green of the sprouting of my heart,
      in the fish-wells of my veins,
    in the shadows of the folds of my shadows.

Enter Long Shadow

eyes like drowned ponds
                              sit down and take nourishment, child
a garment of mold   *dream and ash blended into tea*
sheltering all those others—   *and for your companions*
will it speak to me—is it capable of speech?   *moonbeam candy*
does rot and diamondshine speak?   *sweet birch syrup*
      I'd know   *marbles of petrified dew to play with*
of your pain, Long Shadow,
and how to assuage it.

/// turn me into a forgetting
    [of your offerings we would take]
      swish away pain
        [ash poultice and burnt root of dandelion]
          undo the past, undo us
            [to drink our selves from swamp and swell]
              is that a bargain? do you speak
                to me—are you capable of speech
                  or are you just repeating others:
                    drown its bogblood in water,
                      KILL IT!
                      bury Long Shadow back in deep trenches
                    and not anymore pain
                    [with gratitude, mother]
                  rainbows will rein in wood and field
                and never another war—never another orphan
              torn from its mother's breast—
            never a pulled thread
          in the stitchery of your peace. If only this pest
        were no more—this orphan, this me, this us,
      war-dredged animated stillborn sorrow ///

Such a world is not easily spun.

/// Not easily? How much would you erase?
        How much uproot, unfabric, rip the tapestry off the land—
      a wound here, a pestilence there,
        this child with torn-out limbs, this blind

KILL IT!
    these gouged eyes, this crushed throat
    this village screams forever,
      this marsh conceals corpses—petrified logs
  dead for millennia—
destroy the whole land while you're at it! ///

I refuse
your tale, that the land is fashioned from wars;
I stitched it myself, Long Shadow,
back when the world was young—
of dawn and dew and the joy of pitched tents,
of the braiding of my hair with thread and brass tokens,
of spiked goatmilk and the words sung
in my honor
under the harvesting of the stars

/// and I refuse
  your tale, that the whole land was made
    from sweets like moonbeam candy,
      much less by you. There'd always been wars. Always
        someone writhed in pain, and always
          someone else called the battle beautiful,
            a ravenfeast
              KILL IT!
            adorned with blood-rubies
            bladesong and such nonsense
         that makes children come to rot
         unseen by the likes of you—
      how would you now assuage our pain?
        you say I stole these children: look again,
      babes cut out from slain mothers,
    or else refused life through knife and poison,
  and who would blame
our mothers? not even us ///

I need to think, Long Shadow,
of what you've told me here.
If wrongs cannot be rectified,
how can I help you then?
What good my presence?

/// Oh. You turn away.
  Predictable, now that you know
    we're the children that nobody wants—
      stolen from dead hands, discards
        born maimed, imperfect, torn,
          too damaged for healing—

[of course she turns away]
  but what would you say if I said
    that some of us have been plucked
      hale babes from loving parents
        KILL IT!
      undamaged goods [will she turn away now?]
     Will you turn away now? Or would you stay
    to speak to us, or would it make no difference?
   Immortals and mortals alike
  recoil from maimed children. Easier not to see
 the horrors inflicted upon us, easier to pretend
that nothing bad has happened here.
You cannot change unless you kill.
What need do I have of your changing? ///

I will think of your words and return.

/// I do not believe you.
  [do you believe her?]
   KILL IT!
  return—
 to what purpose?
I do not believe you
I do not believe you
I do not believe you ///

The Journeymaker walks out (II)

I shall stand on your steps, Biruté,
disdained by your toad and beaver, and the child.
How can you stand this—so many truths and none,
  wrapped in mold and silver. No, I do not wish to run
  from it, from *them*—but what can I do? If there's nothing
to *do*, then why does the land cry out to me,
whisper in my ears to seek a healing?

    The river flows. It flows
      past pastures, past meadows of bluebell and periwinkle,
        through the wild tangled thicket
          where the wolf bears down the mother deer.
         Her young will die—and their bones
         grow through with wildflowers.
        Listen, the river flows
       beneath the everchanging moon
      that casts a bitter shadow
      into the waters. Have you seen the boats capsize,
       and weddings end in drownings? Have you seen

bodies
nibbled by the fish, the weeds that grow
from those deaths, the waterlilies?
That, too, is the river.

You say ignore these ills,
for they are only natural?

No.
Listen.
Tell me, what does the river do?
and if it does not do, then what's the point
of rivers? What is the purpose of the moon? The push and pull
of the tides, the incessant changing of it
that changes not at all?

I'm not here to flow, Biruté,
or to contend myself with inaction.
I protect this land with arm and sword,
I fight off those who would wreck it
with plough and battering ram—I protect
the land from worse ills, unspeakable ills,
from the ravening of plagues, and from people
who come from the stars
            despite prohibitions,
to break and kill and strip bare—I fight this.
I bring the dying to my cave
high in the crags, and while nobody watches
I sing the Sword of Healing over mortal wounds,
then let them go, and seek no gratitude. I stitch
paths through wars old and new, and I lead out
those who pray to me. My path is not the moon's,
or the river's, Biruté. If I cannot *do*,
if there's no help that is asked, or even possible,
what is it that you want from me?

Sister, attend.
Cease of your words and attend.
Some wrongs cannot be rectified;
as the river flows,
some wrongs become life.

The Journeymaker stops the world

I lift my arms to the sky,
the shifting stars that ever walk with me—
I know
that I'm to right the wrongs,

to hold the Sword of War safe in its scabbard,
the Sword of Song forever bare and poised to heal;
if that is meaningless, the world
will stop from breath, the rivers from flowing,
the mountains from slow growth, the trees from sap,
the wind from its birth,
the rainbow bridges from their shining,
the bounty of the rain from its harvest—the birds to freeze
mid-flight, and the land to stop from its tilting.

Here, in the forevernow
empty of breath and significance,

I draw again on the sword of bronze.

> I come, Journeymaker,
> though my work is not done,
> I step over emptinesses that froze
> between us, I move without motion
> in this place that is no-place.
>
> Beloved, let me braid your hair
> with threads of sungold and with brass tokens.
> I've forged new ones while I worked
> on other tasks you'd set to me:
> star and skylark,
> raindrops and the wheeling of the sun.

Keddar, an oracle has told me
that your deeds have birthed the wars. Others said
that wars have been here forever,
the whole land marrow-made from them,
and no escape.
There's never been an escape. Day and night I toil
to keep the land safe from harm—I rest
fitfully, I sleep alone
between the bare bones of the earth, I soar
with heaviness. Beloved, I am tired
of these accumulated lives, misdeeds,
of the hurts unhealed, unending
suffering of those I cannot touch, and those I can.
When will there be a forgetting?

> I do not deny my crimes.
> You would not let me if I wanted,
> And I will never want. I led soldiers in battle
> joyfully—I found gladness
> in the vanquishing of my foes,

> the ruination of cities.
> In your service, I remember, and let
> the remembering make me.
> In your service, I work
> to do differently.
> I do not know if that will be enough.
> Some wrongs can never be undone.

They could be quilted over.

> Yes, you could, but you would know
> what's been mended and hidden
> under the newly beautiful cloth.

That too will become soiled
and torn. It always does.
Why should I keep at my stitching?
Why not let
the whole tapestry go, unravel,
fall into dust between my fingers?
Why should the world keep its tilting?

> Love, do you ask,
> how to aid those who refused you,
> and if they keep refusing you, then you will stop
> the world, undo everything?

Do not call me that
if even you will turn against me.

> I will never
> turn against you—
> never again. But these truths
> call out for you. They whisper, they ask:

Go, return

> painful lives, or nothing? Mistakes
> we seek in vain to amend, lives—
> all the rugged breaths, living, surviving—
> crooked, but surviving

Go, return
to the tasks I have set you, between frozen stars

> or a nothingness.

sow peace and reap it with a bloody scythe,
bring back severed threads and call them beautiful.
Return when you're done,
if there's a world to return to,

with the tokens you made for me,
to spin the ashes of my anger
into a gray thread for my hair.

As you command.

The Journeymaker comes to no conclusion

Across the winter grows the shadow long,
across the spring it ripens
to life, and then it comes to devastation.
In summer, the blue of broken eggs
whispers at me, the unborn birds
stolen by lynx and squirrel. That is not the wheel,
I say as the wheel turns. I separate
seasons from unseasons, and yet the pain
fills the bones of the world, until it has always been so.
I heal, they turn away. I walk alone,
I scream, let me do what's required of me
to make these threads sing—but even the threads
that rotted resist their pulling. When I return
to seek Long Shadow—will I speak over
to hush their voice, or attend?
Before I can,
I'll make for me a journey
through rock and wind,
sail the seawater—consider
what I have learned from this, while the world tilts,
and come to no conclusion.
Some wrongs cannot be rectified:
that in itself is a story. That in itself
is the world, much as I resist it: raveled threads
that grow wild from suffering, bloom
in memory's long forgetting, that strive
with riotous colors—

Some wrongs become life.

And then the stars ...

Mack W. Mani

After my father died,
I spent my summers working in
the canneries on the edge of town.

Days of sweat and machinery thunder,
nights full of hard men
and dark country drives
past shadowy fields of sleeping alfalfa.

Weekends spent down at the tavern
trading old stories for the next round
of cheap domestic beer.

Always looking for someone
to take beneath the pepper trees.
Somebody with swagger and words
to fumble at my belt
until we wander back to the bar,
spent and day-drunk,
listening to the rabble of the other men:

Off world, I hear they have real jobs
    and
Once I hit Atmo, I'm never looking back.
    the rally cry of all the boys at drink:
Real life is up there, on the other side of the sky!

Sometimes I look up and wonder …
what's a man like me for?

We all know a guy,
who knows a guy,
who got into The Program.

He got out
    they always say.

And we raise a glass,
whether to his memory,
or his destination
I can't say.

But we take one drink for him,
and throw back the rest for us,
still here on the rock.

They got single women up there?
    one of them asks and everybody laughs.
They got lots of men.
    and they all look to me and have another good one.
Then it's back to the dirty jokes and another round.

I go out for a cigarette.

Nobody smokes anymore,
you have to quit if you want to get anywhere in life.
But the cannery don't care
and Dad smoked 77s until the day he died.

Outside, the May moon splays over the landscape,
and far afield of wild sage,
crickets howl to the darkness of the woods,
where ancient oaks reach up,
into the abyss,
to the most beautiful mess
of twisting purple darkness sky,

      and then the stars....

When you travel out to the colony,
you move so fast
that time slows down around you.

But everyone back on earth
just keeps going,
living and spinning,
keeping up the place.

Out there, you might be anybody.

A streak of light in the sky
and I see a freighter coming home,
bringing back a whole mess of people,
leaving empty space out there, somewhere.

I look down at my smoke, only half done,
when a breeze comes up from the field
and I see something moving out in the darkness ...
something immense and ancient,
lumbering through the night.

Half scared, I retreat back to the safety
of the neon lights and jukebox tune.

I put my cigarette out by the door,
leaving my pack in the gravel.

And I go back inside to say my goodbyes,
and close out my tab.

The night is too long already,
and it is a long way to the place
where I will feel at home.

Interiora II

Alessandro Manzetti

Lightning. The sky is pissed.
The suburb of Rome
is an appetizer of the Purgatory
you can see on the high tide of asphalt,
broken bones, corpses of sirens,
fish bones, and remains of oceans.
It's raining. A dog limps
toward the tent of an abandoned circus,
looking for its master
—a clown without a head or a smile—
with dust on his tongue
and black grease on his rump.

Venus is sleeping
in the yellow building.
She's polluted, as are her dirty sheets.
Her flesh is gone.
Ribs and bones triumph,
waiting for someone else adrift
on her solitary raft,
floating on the edge of reality.

Two hundred dollars for a whole night
with her, with Venus,
with her remains.
Then comes the morning light
—so sharp—
along with the roar of a mower.
The client wakes up
and opens the window.
The stink of gasoline and sadness
enters the room.

He looks out
toward the cemetery of cars
waiting for souls, drivers.
Venus is still in bed.
She's without armor now.
Her teeth sparkle,
showing a skeleton smile.
Her flesh is gone,
along with the subway of her uterus,

the generous glands,
the Byzantine back, and the skin of a mango
—all that she was yesterday.

"Where is my Venus?"
thinks the man leaning against the wall,
eyes popping out of his head.
He tries to break down the door
to get away from that velvet-tongued monster.

Two hundred dollars for a night
with Venus' sister
(Death? Life?),
for her black ring and white bones,
for that damned room,
close, immense,
sealed by an old welder.

The subway swallows its passenger.
All the church bells ring together,
making the ears of the dog prick up,
holding one of its master's bones
in its rotten teeth.

Et je ne pleurais jamais les larmes cicatrisantes magiques; c'est seulement un mensonge joli: Aarne-Thompson Index No. 310

Elizabeth R. McClellan

for Mlle. Charlotte-Rose de Caumont de La Force, erased but not forgotten

Every tower worth its salt
contains a library;
therein lies the undoing of towers.

This is not a boy-story, a babies-story,
it features no brambles, no aimless wandering,
although no dearth of ordinary weeping.

I twirled my tiniest dreadlocks
around my finger, immersed
in tomes of engineering,

every inch the studious schoolgirl

so that the witch smiled, used
less caution, followed

the trail of my locks into
the library, complimented me
when I wove their length into a tighter rope

more easily pushed to one side
of the dark inside stairs. Mostly she was lonely,
never spoke of anyone she saw outside,

and I read to her in the evenings
fables she knew from her girlhood,
though she had to explain what bears were,

the ways of foxes, of rabbits,
show me pictures of what
a river, a knight on horseback looked like,

explain why his skin had no color at all to it,
the illuminated illustrations so bright they hurt my eyes,
even in the dimness of flickering candles.

The witch was old when my mother
was young. By the time my breasts budded,
her stoop was a question mark,

her shuffle whispery as riffling pages.
I figured out the card catalogue on my own.
I think she had forgotten what it contained,

all the innocent books showing types of knots,
the movements of stars as maps to cardinal directions,
how to tell the poison plants from the good,

fulcrums, counterweights,
elegant equations of tensile strength,
cross-braces and structural supports.

She was canny enough not to teach me
much magic, but as she grew frailer,
the simple cantrips to light the torches,

fill her glass with water, or wine,
make the potatoes take root in the dark basement
lightened her load, left more time to rest

between ascents and descents.
By the time she said I was sixteen,
some nights she slept in my bed,

arms too sore, eyes too weak for moonlight rappeling.

I curled around her, sang little songs,
made her tea in the morning

before hauling my hair to the window,
bracing myself against the pain,
which lessened as I grew but was omnipresent,

the cordage from my scalp so thick
the tugs and pulls grew duller,
not so sharp, not as likely to set tears welling

as I read my book and waited
for the extra weight to depart, set to hauling
my pounds of locked curls back through

the narrow casement, coiling them
in the corner, out of my path.
I lifted a section a hundred times a day,

until my arms grew taut as ropes,
ran up and down the stairs
until my thighs burned, waxed strong.

Her sight was failing as it was.
If she noticed, I suppose she assumed
I was just growing like a weed,

flowering in her hothouse care.
She missed, too, the lock I had unwoven
from my rope of hair, breaking each strand

at the root, barely wincing—
when you have borne a woman's weight on your skull,
such pain's a pinprick by comparison

"In a week you will be eighteen, my lovely."
I had to take her word for it, of course,
but counted the days until she came again,

bag full of tiny cakes and beads for my dreads.
I kept her wine cup full, tucked her in—
she did not even notice the hangman's knot of locked hair

I slipped loose around her neck, her murmurs
answered with "more pillows," a sleepy sigh.
She was past dreaming when I tightened it.

By the time she woke, my ropy left arm
was smothering her as she choked on
the locks she had oiled and cooed over.

No coos tonight: thrashing and gasping, betrayed eyes

full of panic. She fought, but I was stronger,
pinned her with my limbs, the rope she'd started

before I remembered anything, before the ladder
that disappeared once my hair reached the ground,
before the tears as my neck bent and scalp burned.

It took longer than it does in books.
It left me with more bruises than I expected.
In death she was even more shrunken.

I closed her eyes and pulled the sheet over her, like a girl in a novel.
I felt like a girl in a novel, like a third-person narrator
watching myself take my actions.

It took three days to haul enough heavy things
up the endless steps, to brace and brace again
until I thought my pile of bookcases, armchairs,

even the bed (now less one stinking corpse)
would hold my weight. Her body
would fertilize the potatoes I wouldn't be there

to harvest. It took another day
to brace my courage, pack the bag
full of my spoils of conquest,

hope my endless practice of knots was enough,
that the engineered jumble and stolen pitons
could stop my free-fall if I plummeted.

I backed out of the narrow window,
the hair that kept me captive now my lifeline.
Halfway down I nearly fainted at how big

the sky really is, outside a picture or
a frame of glass. My head spun, stomach lurched.
I kept my eyes on the stone after that.

At the bottom it took me another three days
to break each hair, one by one, until the north star rose
for me to follow, light-headed, spots of blood

dotting my scalp as the first breeze of my life
caressed my stubbly skull. I marveled at the feel of sand,
a warm floor that shifted grainily under my feet,

walked resolute into a different story,
left only a line of footprints, a dead rope dangling
I hoped no traveler would decide to climb.

Changeling

Lynette Mejía

What started as a game, a hunt
for the curve of your fluid hips
the rough breakers of your knees,
the downy hollow between your legs,
became an abandonment, an abstract idea
of what you'd been only moments
before. Beneath the flannel blanket
we'd mended together, still echoing
with your laughter, its shape
riffing quietly off stones and ceiling plaster,
I searched, and called your name,
and found only my own breath
upon the window.

Now there's nothing left but the taste of you
crackling in the sharp ozone atmosphere,
the air still holding onto your voice,
shards scattered like false breadcrumbs
or sheets snapping crisply in the wind. Sometimes I close
my eyes and I can hear you, singing
in another room, your voice beneath my bones,
a stone set in the hollow of my ribs.

Seven times I waited there, squatting
like a toad in the mud, watching the world die
and be reborn, listening, like a low thing,
for the sound of fairy bells.

And all I've learned is silence;
no one comes this way anymore.

Since then I've kissed the boy asleep,
swept the floors and lit the candle,
my hands growing rough with time and shame
and labor, my only comforts the falling
leaves and the softly sleeping earth.
Sometimes I wonder if you thought of me
as you went out to walk the hills
and stepped into a memory behind the path
of this world, into the home I left
behind to love you. I wonder
whether the air carried my scent,
if the cool touch of her skin was like mine,

if the hunt was as wild as I imagined.

In the beginning I was the pale girl
who dreamed of tasting sun-bright fruit
from the mouth of the darkling Queen,
my pleasure a soft sweetness wrapped
like the anticipation of youth
round a plump pomegranate seed.
Now I'm older, and wiser, my skin lined with care
and the remembrance of your laughter, holding
the knowledge of your kiss,
her delicate, arching hips while I wait,
my heart and hands bitten by salt
and acid tears to bone.

An Unexpected Guest

Lev Mirov

The ghost stood in the hallway and waited for me to speak to him.
I had a creeping sense of him before I opened the door—
a need to keep the lights on, something timid about looking in the mirror at my
    own reflection
(not my reflection, really, but close enough—
the borrowed body I wear on visitations to the South)
that familiar sense of not being alone in my part-time home.
The full moon, fat, obscured, peered through mosquito net clouds
so I saw him brightly in the bathroom doorway:
5 foot 5, wearing drab, scarlet trim on his empty-hanging sleeve.
"Excuse me," the artillery lieutenant said, "can you help me?"

I, who drove in the Motor Transport Corps,
splintered steering wheels with my sweating first hands
patched rubber tires in muddy places
and drove unmarked roads to carry munitions—
I, who moved cannons over heaven and earth
have never told an engineer I can't help, unless I had to.
The war's been over just about a hundred years
I have been lonely in my remembrances, aching and empty at anniversaries,
but old habits die hard, and I only say, "follow me."

In the kitchen my borrowed hands pour red wine, jammy with the taste of plums
and set it before the moon-flooded window.
As is the secret code of soldiers, I light a cigarette but not for myself.
France is coming back in flashes. Anxious, I wonder, why have you come to me now?

Did we serve side by side?
I have no recollection of his face as he clutches the cigarette to his ghost mouth.
I wonder what horrors he will vomit out for us both to live again.
But he does not speak of our shared sorrow.
He does not say: in England I heard you crying for your missing eye
or: you held my remaining hand as the world fell apart
or: we marched in parades when all was said and done and drank after in silence,
     weeping.

He says nothing, drinking wine without even a thank you, desperately thirsty.
I am watching him solidify, almost real enough to touch
as if I could kiss the confused frown away from his mouth.
How did he get in here? How did he find me? Why isn't he one of the ones I know?
Why do only strangers come for me after all this time I have been alone
pretending I am as young as I look, a new name in new towns
borrowing faces since my old body has worn down to nothing without ever
     getting old,
the perpetually cursed pilgrim doomed to live, and live, and live,
when everyone else has died the way that good men ought.

"I'm looking for Amelia," he says, and bitter relief fills me. I don't know any.
Wrong address—none of the ghosts I feed in this complex answer to that name.
"I'm sorry," I say, like that's enough for what I really mean.
"Did she live downtown? Market Street is that way."
He drinks deeply of the wine as if he will finally remember. I hope he does.
I let him out the front door and try not to watch him out the window.
The cigarette at his mouth is still smoldering on the kitchen table.
When I cannot bear how it won't quite burn out, I call a medium I know.

But who knows how to help a ghost when they go wandering?
What can you do but feed the dead, when they draw near you, hungry and full
     of want?
Though the sky is clear of all but gauze, weeping nothing from the wound of night
I hear thunder, like the cannons he once fired and once I moved,
loaded and unloaded on the rail lines in one piece,
broken into parts to haul in the backs of slow trucks named for liberty.
I go back to bed, curling around my lover who is himself half a ghost,
my pianist, who plays songs I knew when I was young
who does not know the color of gas and has never feared the whistle.

Still I am the only one cursed to live long after the rest have gone,
if this is living, me in a borrowed skin, embodiment striking on irregular days
(but of course it is living, if you can still satiate the dead
I still draw the line between us, they still do not count me among their own
and come to me with hungry mouths for what only living memory can give.)
At least tonight, with ghosts afoot, I am not the only one remembering.

Poetry Set: Red Wire, Monsters, Slipknot

A.J. Odasso

Red Wire

Boston Common, 2013. The test
results arrive. Internet geneticists
have decoded my fragility. Blink
at the likelihood of psoriasis. Hold
breath as BRCA1 & 2 show clear,
but say: *Other mutations may exist.*

Time bomb, this body, weeded already
of cysts, endometrium, womb. My chest
fills with doubt, knowing what comes next
will always be the question. My thoughts
turn to introspection: *The parts I want least
are poison-coded in my genes.*

Bleeding, I do not miss. Benign aberrations
are far behind me now. What I must hide
concerns prescience of danger: *My last wish
is the one extraction most likely to be denied.*

Monsters

Your progress through six months of poison
begins. Three days in, you have migraines
to beat the band; three weeks on, your hair
is almost gone. How fast our cells slip

through sheerest trauma is the catch
to our warp and weft. Surgeons say
my healing's too swift; oncologists

prod at your lymph nodes' refusal
to rest. What monsters we are,
mother, remains to be seen—

in the end, what is a wound
but a door through which
blood leaves?

Slipknot

Boston Common, 2015. The PCP-ordered test
comes back conclusive. Medical geneticists
have documented my alterity. BRCA variants
still absent, but another mutation does exist:
CHEK2 is what I carry, and it harbors
a risk too high.

Blink at likelihood of that lump
returning, at the knowledge of alleles
gone awry. Time bomb, this ribcage
strained with doubt. What comes next
is the weight I must ferry. My chest
comprises the ever-unwanted sum
of my parts: *This extraction*
a debt as-yet unpaid.

Bleeding, I will not miss once
the cutting is finished. Absence
of benign aberration abounds: *Denied*
safe passage, grant my fiercest wish.

Halloween

K. A. Opperman

Grim pumpkin faces mock the dark
      With blazing goblin grins:
Each flickeringly brands its mark
On blackened air, mysteriarch
      Of bale that soon begins …
Of weird diablerie that reigns till dawn its throne rewins.

The crimson leaves of autumn flee
      A coming nameless dread:
They swirl through lamplight witchery,
And crawl across the shadowed lea
      Where no one dares to tread,
For fear of devils in the fog, and being faerie-led.

All doors and shutters fast are locked,

The children run and hide.
As midnight time is ticked and tocked,
Their parents peer through cracks unblocked
With fearful eyes and wide,
At dreadful shapes and things with wings that through the shadows glide.

An ill wind slithers in the trees,
Which glowing eyes conceal;
A lantern dances in the breeze,
Illuming hints of blasphemies
Best never to reveal …
Weird shapes that waver by and leave a wake of the Unreal.

Pale corpse-lights flicker in the air
Like embers blown from hell.
Those souls that spy their ghostly flare
Remember stories, and beware
Of what the legends tell. …
They hasten on their way, imperiled by an olden spell.

A sluggish fog engulfs the street
Like smoke from cauldrons vile:
Within it phantom faces fleet,
But floating forth, they oft retreat—
Before a crueler smile!
Those houses without jack-o'-lanterns face a spectral trial.

The elves are sneaking over the sward,
Invisible—but heard;
For on this eve the faerie horde
Awakes over this night to lord,
Whose normal bourns are blurred. …
They curse the scarecrow-guarded crops, and cause the milk to curd.

An owlet's hoot bestirs the fog,
So haunting, desolate;
Somewhere anear the final frog
Quiets its croaks within the bog
Whence came weird sounds of late. …
But when deep Silence settles in, true terror lies in wait.

Behind the rusty, Gothic spears
That fence the graveyard round,
White tapers tipped with fiery tears
Call back the dead of former years
From death's abyss profound:
Amid the mausoleums roaming, restless dead abound.

Grim gargoyles guard the steeple tall,

Wherein is housed the bell;
But in the moonlight's silver thrall,
And autumn dark's phantasmal pall—
When booms the midnight knell—
Those sentinels of sanctity become the fiends of hell!

The moon is seen through filmy clouds,
A skull in moldy soil;
Above the tower, swarming crowds
Of wraiths display their trailing shrouds
Athwart a silver foil;
Whilst on the ground the minions of the moon begin to moil.

Above the distant hinterland,
Whose trees dark secrets screen,
There hangs a faint, arcane command—
A pagan deity seems to stand
Above a blaze pale green....
Old incantations, ancient spells, return on Halloween.

It Begins with A Haunting

Krysada Panusith Phounsiri

a ghost haunts the country of Laos
sieving through jungles
crackling twigs because
it has not yet died
beware of it
the one who drags one foot
while the other rots 20 feet away
shoes made of cast metal
footprints ever so present
in night fall
imprints of bomb shells in mud fields

a phantom roams
plains in Laos
hide your children
its breath reeks of agent orange
its shouts
dynamite flames that dusts away human bones
and bamboo baskets
a stench of wheezing willing to fold
curl
leaves and skins of families who

who hide in forest
till their flesh shrivels
like the lungs of many dead soldiers

the fissures of its face
exposes land mines
crooning a song of torment
through throats of civilians fleeing
on the hair of this
wicket phantom
its hair droops the length
of the Ho Chi Minh trail
hear its whispers

it also cries
moans of a past that begs
to be remembered
clawing trees to spell out its name

the ghost wails pain
filters itself everywhere
whimpering
peeling steal and lead
by the millions
what remains become chains
that burrow into earth
by cluster bombs
big bombs
B-52 bombers dropping
in its tons of U.S. congress approval
in ink
an old friend still alive and well

and under moonlight
refugees run
only to meet more trouble
in camps
they desire to break away
from this ghost and its name
and no one recalls its name
of this

ghoul who rages through
the country of

Laos

melting tendons and flesh

this ghost hungers
for humans
screeching napalm gas on
palms of
guerilla soldiers
american soldiers
and vietcong alike
death does not even remember its name

beware but
tell your children
light the candles and the
incense
the ghost drifts because
no one wants to
know about its name

The Secret War

put this crying soul
of secret history
to rest
recognize
its name
bless this curse
that wants to
name
all the people
it claims
and they too
will remain alive
like mines beneath the soil
seeds of calamity

O Dervish of the Restless Heart

Saba Syed Razvi

1.
Anthem for those Ancestors, or,
Words Astride the Hyphen's Identity

> (after the Kundiman & Kaya Press AWP Seattle Bruce Lee Party)

I don't have, for you, a Bruce Lee poem.

I don't have a poem about an elephant speaking
        in the voice of Ganesh.

I don't have the verse that versus the fundamentalist
        impulse to blow shit up that you don't like.

I don't have one foot in one land or one in another.

I don't know the name for myself that isn't diaspora.

I don't fit enough into one tongue or another,

        but I miss the tongue of that cowboy coming
        home in a big truck,
        still smelling of fracking and the fuel fields.

I don't have, for you, a poem on the occasion of the
        owning of the race of the racists.

I don't have a voice stifled for you beneath an unchosen veil.

I don't have, for you, words that speak your language.

I don't have, for you, words that say "approval"—not
        home, nor from home away from home,
        either.

I don't have, for you a poem, about the nation of my
        name,

        ——just the sinewy sibilance of my fingers,
        scratching out sighs on a page,

        while I think of that good ole once upon a cowboy
        saying "I don't really read such books that often",

        all the while reading stories on my skin, his fingers
        writing silence
                on my sunbrowned sin, and

        my thoughts reaching out to hold his bearded face,
        pull his hips close to mine so that I am filled with a

        forgetfulness
                words that I cannot name, or
        unlearn how to say.

        Those places he has been, I have not; he has seen
        the sands that gave me my name,
                Kan yama kan, Qaf and beyond.

I do not have for you a poem about the nomad in my blood
that knows these sandsongs that I cannot, do not
know how, to say—

Oh, tie-ers of knots, untie my tongue, unknot what
I do not have, for you, a poem about.

2.
American :: Dream

(On the occasion of the departure of forces, US and NATO, after twelve
years of war in Afghanistan)

In the water of the scrying bowl, strings of silver curl into the letters of some
foreign alphabet, letters formed of smoke and fog, of sand and kohl, palimpsests,
of fire, fireless flame, firefly shame, starlight and otherworldly breath, pluming
in the cold of desertscapes. // I dream you, fatigued, in fatigues, flesh charred,
but in tact, singed and covered in soot, but alert and alive, more stunned than
bled, your eyes, smiling – luminous, bright and blue as a drone-ready sky. // I
dream you gathering seeds in the land of pomegranates, scattering them along
the mountainsides, the sandy dunes, the horizon like a lion's mane curling as the
beast startles into some readied stance. // And, as I miss your fingers tracing the
language of my lost tongue along my skin, the words I do not know, bursting into
lush green life inside me, fire and flame and flower petals the color of spring. // I
dream you safe and crossing currents of air and smoke toward an unsettled home,
a waiting home, your hand scattering those gathered seeds with an open hand.
And, when is April like a bride in Spring, the cypresses scenting the breeze? // I
dream that they sprout flesh along barren terrain left behind, hearts, beating fruit,
budding with fear and with frustration, with the anticipation of a coming storm.

3.
Lovesick Wanderer, O Dervish of the Restless Heart

Whirling like the morning's salt-scented breeze, over soft dunes until the sandstorm
tumult in me spins out unembraced across the whole of the horizon

Whirling like the wind over stark sandy dunes until the whole of me fills the horizon
uplifting in maddening tumult, enraptured by the sun's face on every grain of time

Whirling like the rising and rising is a forever forgetting of a lightless descent into arid
desert embrace, sand singing the whole of me to the skeletal skein of horizon

The Coming Dark

Wendy Rathbone

remember
the scents of the sea planets
salt and rain's dew-breath
we brought moisture back to space
in our hair
on our lips

remember
when we made a mini-galaxy from
lasers and holograms
powered by old stardrives
and heat-death
it burned for over a millennium
off the edge of Scorpio

remember
when the Big Attack came
so beautiful
the aliens singing
come into the stranded years
and we will love you forever
enfolding us in the void-silk
of their lullaby nets

remember
that sector called
Meadowspace
where they grew the first ships
to breach the continuum
delicate gossamer candle-hulls
stronger than light
able to host a thousand crew

remember
the eons of war
we circumvented
an accident of lightspeed
the vessel wept
when we forgot to set the helm alarm
after making love
on the pulsing flightdeck

how soon the millions of seasons end

deep in the peach winds of summer-galaxy skies

as the ice hulks approach
faces stare forever
through frozen portholes
angels of winter all dead
bringing our immortality into question

our distress calls fade
in the inked-out depths
as the ships leave
migrating to
some invisible star
searching for new sheens of moons
and auroras

as stars pull away
and light dissolves

—*Wendy Rathbone*

ugly bags of mostly water

Yann Rousselot

in the gas giant i call home there are no capitals—
no territory—frontiers—there are no names at all—
i am we are jovian—there are no verbal tenses—
no modals—timescale is an alien term—
i cannot comprehend—death is not—therefore nor is time—
that which you call winds I call blood flow—
elements of me—are lost as terran metals skim my flesh—
hulls cleaving ice—the ramjets of your explorer vessels—
tear wafts of family from me—
this happening is now—
this happening is all time from then to now and on—
smoke that is me and mine shredded by the thing you call winds—
my mother is my limb—a phantom itch—
so this is death and this is pain—pain is an import—
a data package—a gift—these words your gift to me—
in my home we are what we breathe what we are—
roiling—in the dense metallic hydrogen tori—
rising through cloud strata—i am free—
the familiar press of gigapascals—of critical point heat—
my sisters and brothers bleed into me—
we roar along the rust belts—the great red spot—

the polar vortex—the caress of solar flares—
ruffle the molten methane and ammonia oceans of me—
the storm-riven non-surface of me and mine—
that which you call skin—
a threadbare term to describe where i stop and others begin—
a terran distinction—i am we are in a supercritical fluid state—
you cannot comprehend—yet you try—
your probes plunge into me from afar—
with them parts of me travel to the small terran blue dot—
i am broken down and remade—laboratory is the term—
prison is the semantic reference point—
i exhale my thoughts which you inhale—digest—ignore—
you strange liquids in flexible envelopes—
the prisons you call skin—
poke—dissect—heat and cool the elements of me—
your questions—a torture—
thrown across the Kelvin scale—
irradiated—electromagnetised—
lack of sentience boiled down to a missing link—
a dead end in the act of communication—
i am released for lack of commercial potential—
exhaled by the containers of liquid who return to their homes—
within frontiers—within concrete boxes—
within flexible bags of skin—
i am a lonely cloud in terran skies and it is so cold here—
the cirrus and nimbus trawlers are mindless—
akin to the rock at the core of my jovian world—
mobile and mindless—sentience a curse—
time—i now comprehend—
it is slow and so cold below the critical point—
i long for home
gravity the unbreakable shackle to this planet—
a curse alike to sentience and skin—
skin the unbreakable shackle to the thing you call body—
your gift to me—i curse you and your words that make the world—
all of you—ugly bags of mostly water—

The Noble Torturer

Sofia Samatar

The Noble Torturer arrives with tools and a melancholy expression. He is in pain.
He is both victimizer and victim. Usually he belongs to some sort of underclass.

He could have been you. He is pitted against the government he serves.

The Noble Torturer has father issues. His father is the US government. His father is cruel. His father has forced him to commit evil acts. This experience has given him lasting trauma, but it has also equipped him with formidable skills. Quite often, the Noble Torturer is now working against the government. He's gone rogue. He has stolen his father's car and left the state. He hopes his father cries at the angry note he tacked to the kitchen door. I HATE YOU! Inside, the Noble Torturer is just a little boy.

The Noble Torturer has many facets; this is why he glitters. People call him a "complex character" although he has no depth.

He is both pro-war and anti-war; therefore, everyone loves him. People of all political persuasions succumb to his spell.

The Noble Torturer is dependable. He will definitely make you feel something.

The Noble Torturer is working on an elevated level of manpain. It's far more sophisticated than the manpain experienced by, for example, Russell Crowe's character in that *Gladiator* movie. The gladiator's wife and child were murdered, crucified I think, and his wife was raped "again and again" as Joaquim Phoenix's character put it, and the gladiator's manpain grew so intense that it produced an entire movie, but it's still nothing compared to the Noble Torturer's manpain! The Noble Torturer's manpain is located entirely within himself. It doesn't depend on the suffering of someone else. Unless you count the torture victims, but who's counting them? The Noble Torturer's pain eclipses all other agonies.

The Noble Torturer is both the man crying in the dirt and the dead woman hanging from the eaves of the house.

Like a king on a playing card, he has two heads.

The Noble Torturer provides his own sunset. He rides into himself.

Mostly importantly, the Noble Torturer is an artist. The camera dwells on his tool set. He has blunt tools and delicate ones, like a painter with different brushes. The Noble Torturer is a virtuoso of pain. He usually explains to his victim that he's extremely good at his job. Of course this terrifies the victim. It also marks the Nobel Torturer as a gifted person, one set apart by his skill. The Noble Torturer is glorified in his marvelous dexterity and in his marvelous sorrow.

The Noble Torturer belongs to a skilled elite. You can't just be born into that kind of expertise! You have to earn it! With his often homely instruments (pliers, drills) the Noble Torturer combines the Great Artist with the Guy Next Door.

This dwelling on his artistry—the way the camera lingers—reveals the true purpose of the Noble Torturer. His purpose is the aestheticization of war. More specifically, it is the aestheticization of trauma.

The Noble Torturer makes trauma beautiful.

This is a message that goes beyond forgiveness. It's not that we forgive you for the terrible things you've done. It's that we love you for them and we want you to continue, we want you to go on to the point of death. If you've tortured for your country, if you wake every night with a racing heart, if you suffer from panic attacks in the grocery store, you must understand that you are now your father's favorite child. The camera loves you. Everybody loves you.

Trauma becomes melancholy, therefore attractive. In fact it's kind of hot.

The Noble Torturer admits everything. He knows he's been very bad.

When he looks in your eyes, you both know he'll do it again.

He has every right.

He is justified through injustice: that's his magic.

The more he hurts you, the less important your pain becomes. Your pain is absorbed into his, gathered to it, blended with it, dissolved. When he cuts you, you exist only in the cut. You are all surface, all exterior, while his interior develops. He goes on the journey of pain with you, but as your pain makes you more emphatically a body, his pain gives him something resembling a soul. His personhood advances in direct proportion to your thingness. This is why you are perfect for each other.

There's a lot of blood. Afterward, the Noble Torturer sings in the shower. You can hear him singing while you lie and wait. You don't know what you're waiting for. He sings: *The worse things are, the better they are. Pain is beautiful. War is beautiful.*

Keziah

Ann K. Schwader

> ... *and who can say what underlies the old tales of broomstick rides through the night?*
> —H.P. Lovecraft, "The Dreams in the Witch House"

I. How It Began

She knew no God. The Devil, very well:
From every neighbor's narrowed prying eyes
A hint of brimstone shone. No further hell
Required for any woman grown too wise
With age, too solitary, & too poor
For much regard or grudging charity
Dispensed by goodwives from their kitchen doors,

With hissings to depart & leave them be.

No humble supplicant, she muttered dark
Beneath her breath as speculation spread
From tongue to idle tongue that she was marked
By witchery. Such superstitious dread
Excused their cruelty—or so they claimed—
Till she put nameless power to that name.

II. The White Stone

None living knew its origins. A stone
As leprous as the moon of some lost world,
It rose against the dark like vengeance hurled
From utter Void. She came to it alone
As seekers must, dream-driven to pursue
Deliverance by means beyond the pale
Provisioning of nature, & prevail
Against her enemies, though hell ensued.

Her answer slipped like shadow through the face
Of that great stone: a stranger robed in night
Itself, yet blacker still. He held a book
Filled with malignant magicks, time & space
Alike defiled … & as he bade her write
Her name in blood within, the heavens shook.

III. Nahab

Constrained no longer by the laws of man,
She wandered as she willed, & what she wrought
On certain Sabbats would not be forgot
In Arkham town for centuries. Tales ran
From house to house of horrors scarcely fit
For whispering: a missing infant's cry
Cut short in shadows, cattle bled out dry
By needle teeth. Half frightened from their wits,
Her neighbors sent to Salem. Strangers came
With sacred texts, & weapons freshly blessed
To search their alleys for a witch's nest—
Yet when they battered down her attic door,
A clamoring of witnesses proclaimed
What lay beyond was nothing seen before.

IV. Under Pressure

She told old Hathorne everything, at last:
The hideous fragility of space
Diaphanous as mist, through which she passed
Upon the Black Man's errands. Any place
Might open on a coven, & each rite
Conceal within its crude simplicity
Some undertone of Chaos, put to flight
Delusions of divine felicity …

He never let her finish. Proudly blind,
He prattled on about the Tempter's wiles,
So fatal to a weak & female mind.
His prisoner spat blood at him—then smiled,
Appearing not to notice when he said
She'd hang at cock-crow, by the neck, till dead.

V. Through Certain Angles

In blood lies power. By this primal law,
Mere curves & angles daubed on stone became
A well-mapped passage through our mundane frame
Of space to points *outside*. Those poisoned claws
Called justice could not touch her as she slipped
Between dimension-gates to heed the call
Pulsating out from that abyss where all
Persuasions & equations lose their grip
Upon reality. At length, a shrill
& mindless piping rose; yet as she knelt
Before her daemon-sultan on His throne
Of shattered stars, He knew her not until
She offered up her secret name—& felt
Herself delivered, chosen as His own.

VI. Of What Remained

They came for her at dawn, but found that cell
As empty as their understanding. Smeared
On every surface, figures rose & fell
Through ruptured space: the calculus of fear
Laid forth in gore. Her gaoler stayed behind
A fatal moment longer—till one heap
Of straw disclosed the ruin of his mind,

Likewise all reasoned speech or peaceful sleep.

Whatever scuttled from that fetid bed
Was neither rat, nor mouse, nor any beast
Begotten on this planet. Nightmare-bred,
It glared up from its interrupted feast
Amid a charnel-heap of splintered bones,
& cursed his soul to hell … in human tones.

Adarna

M. Sereno

> *May isang ibong maganda*
> *ang pangalan ay Adarna,*
> *cun marinig mong magcantá*
> *ang saquít mo'i, guiguinhaua.*
> —from *Ibong Adarna*, author unknown

Princess, they say: find her in the garden of bone,
feeding hearts to the soil. Say: she belongs to the dark.
The dark has her. Yes. I am here. Come closer.
I have strung you a ladder of branches to climb
to the teeth of the moon. Come up and I shall sing to you:
chirruping paniki, kuliglig, salagubang beating greeting
in notes of chitin, dark gold. Press soles flat onto granite spine,
rock-choked chest. Climb grasping, clenched fists bleeding
sharp kalamansi onto the rocks of my garden, these bodies
laid open to the bone. The tao with their hearts exposed—
what is left to you but to become stone? Flesh now food
for my dream-eyed waling-waling, violet mouths open
on galaxies of alitaptap. I will not tell you, princess,
do not be afraid. Be afraid, and swallow your fear.
For you I will siphon a new song from my throat
in copper and wet limestone. Come to me closed,
moon-bright. Open to talons gleaming with blood drawn
from entrails massed, sampaguita's sweet swell. Put out
your tongue—heto, katotohanan. Oo, mapait. Bakit ka narito?
Ano ang hinahanap mo?

Halika. Climb higher, though gravity calls
like your own mother. Monsters shall beckon—
you must resist. Push fingers hard into salt, grip kampilan
in silver-sweating palm, panting sulfur: your land's char.

Yet look at you. Spine a drawn bow aimed at my chest,
salvation burning its ember on your brow. Would you
redeem stone corpses for flesh, surrender my garden
to tao's hands, tie me to you, a feathered talisman of life?
What is the weight of Adarna's meat on your kingdom's scales?
Anak ng tao, consuming only delays being consumed:
hunger comes for us all, its smile the blazing sun. As men did,
burning in need to possess glory, body, what was
not theirs to claim. See: they stand here still.

Sit with me, princess. Not dawn yet, sawa coiling forests
deep and green around our feet, and still so much to feast on.
I will trade their lives for your close arms, the bright spears
lancing from your eyes. It is not true what they say
about the dark: you know how shadows protect,
shielding flesh uneaten from the teeth of men. So it is
even with monsters. I was born in flame. Out of sun's blood,
a fierce womb burnished gold from when araw meant
radiance and not a father's killing blow. Birthed to hiwaga,
rhythm, burning—and you would have my music, take me back
to warble life into a ruler's limbs, cage me to carol enchantment
over your lands. Suck me dry of all the fruits of song
as one tears meat from bone, inhaling its marrow.
Tao, prinsesa, daughter of dry soil: conquer the thighs
of the earth, surmount the black cheeks of smoke-crowned
volcanoes. But seek not my voice. Grasp not this song.
It will cut off your fingers, shatter your bones:
sharper than slicing through sinew, this storm-sound,
tempest in halimaw's throat, all the fury of sigwa, unos,
bagyo—then the silences of bundok shouldering upward,
their mineral strength. Lindol at alon:
lulunurin ka, lalamunin. Aawit ako at guguho
ang iyong mundo. Turn back, child of ruin.
Princess, this is what they will not say:
song is blood.

Hear now of my mothers. Crouching in my ribcage
of brittle branches, the wind's fingers sign of the women
who sang before the white armies came. Who would say:
halika, halika. Kumain ka na ba? Oh smoke, crackle of fire!
Floating above, clear music, the hum as fingers peeled
eggs into shining wholeness, stripping chicken bones
down to the last small frailty, sifting through rice for root,
stone, soil. Women who buried secret coin in wrinkles,
palms: pain to keep awake. Ways to keep on living
until your back bristles with sharpened spears, and
your veins map everything you endured as bargain for

another breath. To yield, spine bowing to brutal force,
or to die. To resist in each silent stitching
of isip—salita—gawa—all yours. To hide old names
under tongue's fury, dark slivers in your wrists.
To hold on to brown skin: to shed blood for it.
Babae is only another name for a strength
that does not shatter, just as eating is the throat-pulse
of love. We endure our desire: I was burnt up by it,
branded by what I wanted long before
it was lawful for me to know want. Princess, yes—
even with monsters. The tongue your mother lost,
did she swallow it to feed her hunger, or to forfeit
a crimson choking? Bakit ka narito? Sino
ang hinahanap mo? To enter my garden
you have dared rivers' flood-gorged bellies,
buwaya's jaws, swimming on and waiting
for the chance to break the surface, gulp in air.
Only to redeem warriors bulging with a hollow
possession. Is this your desire? It is the tao's way
to trade one life for another, lesser body for greater,
though we know the scales are false. Here, a wound
on your arm; here a deeper one: remembering how
you suffocated in want, how you hid your teeth sinking
into deep sweetness, your nails opening mouths
to redden flesh. Why are you here? Who do you seek?
Not the men drunk on empire lapping at your seas,
nor the false radiance of swords to spite fear. Nor
the choice: to become dry bone. To be swallowed
by it. The truth bitter on your tongue, princess,
and gore rimming your lips indelible.
There is a song that must be sung
to show that it is no punishment
that we survive.

See: the sky lightens, gilds the brows of these
my stone hunters. What gift shall I grant you?
I cannot spare you. None of us are spared.
So my sisters went, the night-tressed aswang.
So my mothers. So now I.
Put out your hand. Halika. We are still here.
Our voices rise meticulous into the air, halimaw
babae gamit ari-arian, like fragrance from crushed
sampaguita. Who taught you not to sing? Do you hear
stone, cracking? Look, the trees awake, reaching
for the infant sun, clawing at its pale yellow egg
before it births immensity. The air thickening

with silver-wreathed planets and unstained stone,
while the dark surrenders to clouds banked in misty gold.
Doom licks at my chin. Princess, you have wars to win,
spellbound men to save, a homecoming weighted
with shattered rock and triumph over monstrous Adarna.
In the distance I can smell the hot reek
of the tao's cages, scorched grass, ashes.
No one will spare us. But know this, anak:
you can swallow drought and bone—not
be consumed in it. Princess, a song
cannot do all things. A song
is a blade is a blossom is
a swallowed sun.
I do not desire to die. Yet
if we must die,
we go into death
singing.

Kumain ka na ba? Halika, halika.
Lift your head. Kiss my mouth.
I'll open you up:
devour me.

Twenty Years

Christina Sng

The hovercraft loomed,
A silent sentinel watching
Over me and my little ones,
Waiting to take us
To a new home,

A new life.
Away from our dying planet,
Where the rising seas
Have washed away the cities,
Drowning all life, and humanity.

The promise was
A blue-green planet
Twenty light years away.
The caveat, we had to
Leave our old behind.

I held my mother's hand,

Wrinkled and dry, now
Damp with tears
Free-falling from her face.
And Papa

Standing beside her,
Our rock, full of emotion
He would never show
But a glisten in his eyes,
A trick of the light.

She grazed my cheek
With the soft back of her hand,
Like she did when I was little.
Dear girl, we are eighty.
We have lived.

Even if we could go,
We would not live to see
The new world. It would be
Twenty years in a ship.
Death on a ship.

I grew desperate, tears
Blinding. I grasped her hand
Tighter. We could stay.
The planet is a pipe dream.
We might not breathe.

Here, we can fish,
Live in the mountains.
We can find a way.
I would rather twenty years
Here with you

Than eternity in a metal box
Full of empty promises.
Papa's hand fell gently
On my shoulder. Child,
He said. You must think

Of them. His eyes turned
To my children, both
Bright eyed and happy,
Dancing around their
Grandparents, oblivious

To the agony we felt.
I held his eyes, and saw

Conflict and sadness
And a determination
To do what was right.

As did I.

I nodded to the pilot
Who saluted and left.
I embraced my mother
And father, and held
My children tight.

Together we watched
The hovercraft depart.
Mama said, now we
Have twenty years
Together.

No, I said.
We have forever.

The Woman in the Coffee Shop

Christina Sng

She was elegant, more
Graceful than a swan,
Neck like the pale white
Inner bark of a young tree.

Her hair was onyx, woven
Like black dragon beard candy
Onto her head, held only
By a single wooden chopstick.

Oak, I recognised. Not
From around here. Just like her,
An old-world hardened weariness
That came only with age. Great age.

Yet she looked only 35,
Face pale and unlined, her ears
Distractingly almost elven. And
Her ebony eyes—

Abyssal,
Deeper than death;
Maelstroms opening gateways

To unknown alternate universes.

She turned those eyes on me now,
Staring piercingly into mine.
I must have frowned, for her lips
Parted into a smile.

"Which one is he?"
She asked, in a soft whisper.
I turned my eyes to him,
Sitting nonchalantly

Four tables away,
Counting his 4D tickets
And drinking *teh tarik*.
She looked back at me

With those peerless eyes
And nodded.
Time froze
In that instant.

And everyone in the coffee shop
Along with it: patrons with coffee
Cups in hand; a man labouring
A heavy tray, pausing mid-step

As if to collect his thoughts;
A *prata* suspended in the air,
Swirled like a faraway
Infinite galaxy;

Saffron droplets
Freeze framed above
A child's plate beside me,
Her face full of glee.

It would be her first taste of curry:
Her mother capturing the moment
While grandma beamed proudly
And big sister sipped her tea.

I did not see the chopstick
Pierce his throat till
The world unfroze
And the first screams began.

When I turned, she was gone.
Later, by Papa's bedside,
I held his still hand, stroked

His unruly hair from his face.

"Mama is avenged," I told him.
"Please wake up now. Please."
His breath quickened. I knew
He heard me. I thought of

The woman in the shop
And how she appeared
Out of nowhere to help me.
What did she want?

And why did she wear
My dead mother's face?

The Iterative Nature of the Magical Discovery Process

Bogi Takács

for {J, M}

Spellwords: LĀM WĒ AWĀN

Mairu:

We're testing the patience of jellyfish;
Eyawan dips ankles, hands in the water
as she struggles to maintain altitude.
The spell should be technically correct,
she just has difficulty with power.
I push the oft-heard words away from myself:
       humans are not supposed to fly.

Eyawan:

Along a straight line; how simple,
I thought, and yet how to persist
in this heated constantly dragging-
draining spellsheath around me
I do not know! But Mairu could—

Mairu:

She resists to ask until she falls,
clambers out of the shallow seawater
grimacing, jellyfish-stung.

Together we have enough magic—
I only ask if I could watch from below,
for I am dearly afraid of the sky.

Eyawan:

Yes! I am pulled along as if
on a string, these breathrending
ever-hastening speeds
make my blood steam! Yes—
but I cannot go higher,
I nudge my body against the air
I despair—will I forever
trail the watersurface, never to
rise higher, will I be fated
to this distasteful imitation,
a pretend-seagull cawing in vain?

Mairu:

We must rethink the spellwords.

Spellwords: LĀM WĒ LĀM

Eyawan:

I shrug, ignore the smiles giggles
that trail us like water drips
in our footsteps. Kids run after us
race from the hilltops and squeal
in delight. Possibility-churn in
my thoughts, an overabundance
of fresh approaches—I shall not be
distracted, I shall *not*—

Mairu:

The bristly fisherfolk truly like us:
two haphazard women from the city
who hug and kiss with a passion.
They are not intimidated,
do not whisper or point fingers,
two such strong mages, not
in a hundred years—I grew weary
of the chatter in the Academy.

I wanted to *work*, and Eyawan likewise:
even now, walking along the
dirt path with chin held high,
I can feel the feverish thought-churn
inside her unruly head.

Eyawan:

Wait—ahead lies a pattern
of relating a concept to itself
binding it together one to one.
Rubberstrings will snap me
into the clouds when we try this—
        Mairu, Mairu, can it be today?

Mairu:

After a hearty fish-stew we rush back
to the shore, Eyawan already plotting.
My stomach is too complacent and full,
but her enthusiasm helps draw the magic
from within my chest. She swings up
into the air, at a familiar angle:
one-eighth of a circle as they measure
in the Academy. She laughs and whoops,
disappears into the sky. Fear grips me
for a moment, but she keeps
steadily drawing on my magic,
therefore she must be all right.
She reappears at a similar, descending angle—
did she reverse the spell? Hmm ...
        Beloved, can we change
        just a few words
        and thus change the steepness?

Eyawan:

I love you. I really need to sleep.

Spellwords: LĀM WĒ AWĀN LĀM

Mairu:

My construction, my concept this time?
We complement each other and sometimes

we find it hard to tell us apart—
even though Eyawan is brusque and I am
mild and stolid, on occasion even boring.
Our handiwork merges smoothly.

Eyawan:

Twice as high, twice as fast, twice twice
I can just multiply, increase, soar
mock the sea-creatures from above,
twist and corkscrew around my axis
as the spell drives me up like an arrow
in a straight line steeper than last time.
This, this is improvement,
the sheer force of iteration that must
eventually produce a breakthrough—
this is what drives me onward.

Mairu:

Persistence is the key that opens this lock.
My magic is smooth and flat like the islands,
and as it joins with Eyawan's and pulls her
ever higher, I hiss between my teeth—
I close my eyes to feel the wind against her face.

Spellwords: LĀM WĒ LĀM AWĀN-WĒ LĀM

Eyawan:

We roast onions I munch, the sweet taste
splattering in my mouth and we muse,
triumph must be so close as to touch—oh
   why does it have to be a straight line
   why
   if we use a concept to describe the slope
   we can also fill that slot
   with the concept itself
   we can, we can—

Mairu:

Sometimes I'd just like to eat,
but this time I'm curious, eager
to see what our new set
of spellwords brings.
We build science out of nothing.

A new, different world—
populated by shared ideas
and filled with gasping delight.

Eyawan:

Ever-curving skyward, this falling
sunward grips me as I spread
arms to feel the resistance of air
on my skin—I cry with the release
of joy, mutual success, I sense
Mairu down below stretching out
hands toward me and smiling, I, I —

Mairu:

Eyawan, it's me!

Eyawan:

We.
       I flatten, fall back-forward,
splosh into sea like a lost firework —
these curves and arcs are tricky!
I spit out saltwater and cuss.
Yes, we did it!

Mairu:

This embrace, this dance
in the sticky-warm sea
is a pearl of memory
I shall cherish, I know —
but my mind already works
on formulating the next step,
and with Eyawan it's the same.
We join hands, drag each other
to the rough-grained sand,
lie there panting as the grit
insinuates itself into fabric—
I'll have plenty to wash.
Now, we pledge to each other:
       Tomorrow, we begin again.

The poem references János Bolyai's famous dictum: "Out of nothing, I created a new,
different world."

Describing the mathematical functions using current Earth conventions is an exercise left to the reader. Solutions below …

$x \to 2$

$x \to x$

$x \to 2x$

$x \to x^2$

A Love in Twelve Feathers

Shveta Thakrar

for Mike Allen

First feather

Girl for sale
Garbed in blues and greens
Framed in a circle of filigree
Dangling from a fine gold chain

Your knife hooked as a bird's beak,
My love,
You carved out my heart
And drew it back in
With pen and pigment
And placed it under glass
For all to see

Second feather

In the strolling park where you painted
Just beneath the pomegranates
I strummed my sarangi
Each string a strand of long black hair
Each note a drop of blood

It hurts, it hurts
To be alone
A dark sky without a moon

But no one heard my song
Amidst the birdcalls,
My love—
Except for you

Third feather

A god you were
With a single feather in your crown
Your devotee
Chanting your hallowed name
In hushed tones
Waving my heart on a silver tray
Ringed with marigolds and sindoor-red roses
Before your statue on the shrine:

"O Lord, I beg you,
Accept this humblest of offerings!"

In the end, you did
And now you must eat from my hand
For always

Fourth feather

All the peacocks preened around you:
"Meh-aao, meh-aao!"
I laughed, for they might call down the rain
Yet what thunderhead
No matter how dark
How bitter and dismal
Could truly hide
The sun's resplendent face?

Fifth feather

"Art is forever," you whispered
Lifting your brush
Brushing my hand
"Like love.
A moment made eternity."

"Then paint me," I pleaded
"I will dance for you, sing for you.
Only paint me bright and bold."

You studied me, then flashed
A smile like salty secrets
An appraiser's smile:
How much, the value of this singular jewel?

My smile was all intrigue:
More than all the diamonds

More than all the pomegranates
More than all the peacocks in the world.

"Yes," you said, and began

Sixth feather

We were to wed
My heart, your hand
When the parched river drank you down
Leaving me only your pendant
With my portrait

I could not live

Forgive me, my love
A peacock was all I could manage

Seventh feather

The quill so sharp against my skin
Drawing blood as you drew my cheekbones
The kajal over my eyes
The sorrow below my breast

Your lost breath, my spilled tears:
The spell is cast

Eighth feather

You had me eating out of your hand,
My love,
Just as if I were the bird and you—
You the master, always

Yet I was the one with the magic
And I learned just how suddenly
Lovebirds forget to fly
When forced to part

Ninth feather

Everything must eat
It is a law of our world

Everything must eat:
You, the peacocks, I
Even art demands to be fed

An artist must sacrifice
For his muse
Not only tears and time
But souls and selves

Oh, my love,
You knew that going in
As did I

Sometimes the muse, too,
Must sacrifice herself for the artist

Tenth feather

You drew me so well, my love,
That I woke from death in my own likeness
Then, when my charm took effect
I drew you

My love, my love, did you really think
That whatever form you wore
In your next life—
Bird, blossom, or beast—
I would not find you again?

Eleventh feather

There is no eleventh feather
Enchantments, too, must be nourished

Twelfth feather

Twelve feathers minus one make a fan
Like the one I waved in your direction
On the days made of fire and dust
A peacock's all-seeing eyes

They watch me now
As you, my love,
Won back from the thirsty river
And soundly preserved behind the glass
Of the pendant you once gave me,
Forever bend forward to peck seeds
From the bowl of my curved palm
Under my tenderest of smiles

The poem was written in conjunction with the necklace by Meenoo Mishra, which can
be viewed with the poem at strangehorizons.com/2015/20151019/thakrar-p.shtml

A Butterfly in Carcosa

D. J. Tyrer

They say that a butterfly
Flapping its wings
Can change the weather elsewhere
But what peculiar effects
Might a butterfly's wingbeats cause
When it flits through Carcosa?
A lone yellow butterfly
Of the sort said to be the archetype
Of that insect class
Flutters through shadowed streets
Like a lone autumn leaf.
From between soaring towers
A Purple Emperor proudly flies out
The two butterflies ignore each other
Just flit through darkening alleyways
As the twin suns set
Passing on their separate ways
As night falls, a moth takes flight
Whilst the butterfly seeks shelter
In an abandoned graveyard.
What peculiar sights
Might that moth perceive
As it flits through Carcosa?
Other things take flight
Between the soaring towers
On that moonless night
Things that call Carcosa home
And on earth are unknown.
When the twin suns rise
That metaphor once more takes flight
Soaring through ruddy skies.
As a butterfly is born
From a cocoon
So might one identity
Break free from within another.
The curse of Carcosa
Is freedom.
But is freedom what you want?
The truth can set you free
But the truth can consume you
And burn you up.

The touch of Carcosa
Transforms you.
But can you live with it
Your true identity
Exposed to the world
To ridicule?
So the cocoon cracks open
To release the real you
Who had been hidden within.
Emerging into the light
Of twin suns above a lake
The real you wanders
Wide-eyed through Carcosa.
Past soaring towers you stumble
Gazing upward incredulously
Unable to comprehend
The majesty of Carcosa.
Sudden movement startles you
And you turn to see a butterfly
Flitting past you down the street.
Curious, you follow.
The butterfly leads you
Through ancient winding streets
Rimed with an aeon's tears.
Finally, you reach a meadow
On the shore of that lake
Cloudy and strange.
As you step into that meadow
A thousand butterflies take flight
Joining their fellow in the air
No longer alone
But part of a reversed autumnal fall
Of yellow leaves
Engulfing you in golden haze
As they surround you
Submerge you
Until all is infinite yellow
And you find yourself falling
Into an eternity of yellow
Swallowed whole
By the dancing host
Of butterflies.
Embraced.
Yellow.
Free.

Rhysling Award Winners 1978–2015

1978	Long	Gene Wolfe	"The Computer Iterates the Greater Trumps"
	Short	Duane Ackerson	"The Starman"
	(tie)	Sonya Dorman	"Corruption of Metals"
		Andrew Joron	"Asleep in the Arms of Mother Night"
1979	Long	Michael Bishop	"For the Lady of a Physicist"
	Short	Duane Ackerson	"Fatalities"
	(tie)	Steve Eng	"Storybooks and Treasure Maps"
1980	Long	Andrew Joron	"The Sonic Flowerfall of Primes"
	Short	Robert Frazier	"Encased in the Amber of Eternity"
	(tie)	Peter Payack	"The Migration of Darkness"
1981	Long	Thomas M. Disch	"On Science Fiction"
	Short	Ken Duffin	"Meeting Place"
1982	Long	Ursula K. Le Guin	"The Well of Baln"
	Short	Raymond DiZazzo	"On the Speed of Sight"
1983	Long	Adam Cornford	"Your Time and You: A Neoprole's Dating Guide"
	Short	Alan P. Lightman	"In Computers"
1984	Long	Joe Haldeman	"Saul's Death: Two Sestinas"
	Short	Helen Ehrlich	"Two Sonnets"
1985	Long	Siv Cedering	"Letter from Caroline Herschel (1750–1848)"
	Short	Bruce Boston	"For Spacers Snarled in the Hair of Comets"
1986	Long	Andrew Joron	"Shipwrecked on Destiny Five"
	Short	Susan Palwick	"The Neighbor's Wife"
1987	Long	W. Gregory Stewart	"Daedalus"
	Short	Jonathan V. Post	"Before the Big Bang: News from the Hubble Large Space Telescope"
	(tie)	John Calvin Rezmerski	"A Dream of Heredity"
1988	Long	Lucius Shepard	"White Trains"
	Short	Bruce Boston	"The Nightmare Collector"
	(tie)	Suzette Haden Elgin	"Rocky Road to Hoe"
1989	Long	Bruce Boston	"In the Darkened Hours"
	(tie)	John M. Ford	"Winter Solstice, Camelot Station"
	Short	Robert Frazier	"Salinity"
1990	Long	Patrick McKinnon	"dear spacemen"
	Short	G. Sutton Breiding	"Epitaph for Dreams"

1991	Long	David Memmott	"The Aging Cryonicist in the Arms of His Mistress Contemplates the Survival of the Species While the Phoenix Is Consumed by Fire"
	Short	Joe Haldeman	"Eighteen Years Old, October Eleventh"
1992	Long	W. Gregory Stewart	"the button and what you know"
	Short	David Lunde	"Song of the Martian Cricket"
1993	Long	William J. Daciuk	"To Be from Earth"
	Short	Jane Yolen	"Will"
1994	Long	W. Gregory Stewart and Robert Frazier	"Basement Flats: Redefining the Burgess Shale"
	Short	Bruce Boston	"Spacer's Compass"
	(tie)	Jeff VanderMeer	"Flight Is for Those Who Have Not Yet Crossed Over"
1995	Long	David Lunde	"Pilot, Pilot"
	Short	Dan Raphael	"Skin of Glass"
1996	Long	Margaret B. Simon	"Variants of the Obsolete"
	Short	Bruce Boston	"Future Present: A Lesson in Expectation"
1997	Long	Terry A. Garey	"Spotting UFOs While Canning Tomatoes"
	Short	W. Gregory Stewart	"Day Omega"
1998	Long	Laurel Winter	"why goldfish shouldn't use power tools"
	Short	John Grey	"Explaining Frankenstein to His Mother"
1999	Long	Bruce Boston	"Confessions of a Body Thief"
	Short	Laurel Winter	"egg horror poem"
2000	Long	Geoffrey A. Landis	"Christmas (after we all get time machines)"
	Short	Rebecca Marjesdatter	"Grimoire"
2001	Long	Joe Haldeman	"January Fires"
	Short	Bruce Boston	"My Wife Returns as She Would Have It"
2002	Long	Lawrence Schimel	"How to Make a Human"
	Short	William John Watkins	"We Die as Angels"
2003	Long	Charles Saplak and Mike Allen	"Epochs in Exile: A Fantasy Trilogy"
	(tie)	Sonya Taaffe	"Matlacihuatl's Gift"
	Short	Ruth Berman	"Potherb Gardening"
2004	Long	Theodora Goss	"Octavia Is Lost in the Hall of Masks"
	Short	Roger Dutcher	"Just Distance"

2005	Long	Tim Pratt	"Soul Searching"
	Short	Greg Beatty	"No Ruined Lunar City"
2006	Long	Kendall Evans and David C. Kopaska-Merkel	"The Tin Men"
	Short	Mike Allen	"The Strip Search"
2007	Long	Mike Allen	"The Journey to Kailash"
	Short	Rich Ristow	"The Graven Idol's Godheart"
2008	Long	Catherynne M. Valente	"The Seven Devils of Central California"
	Short	F. J. Bergmann	"Eating Light"
2009	Long	Geoffrey A. Landis	"Search"
	Short	Amal El-Mohtar	"Song for an Ancient City"
2010	Long	Kendall Evans and Samantha Henderson	"In the Astronaut Asylum"
	Short	Ann K. Schwader	"To Theia"
2011	Long	C. S. E. Cooney	"The Sea King's Second Bride"
	Short	Amal El-Mohtar	"Peach-Creamed Honey"
2012	Long	Megan Arkenberg	"The Curator Speaks in the Department of Dead Languages"
	Short	Shira Lipkin	"The Library, After"
2013	Long	Andrew Robbert Sutton	"Into Flight"
	Short	Terry Garey	"The Cat Star"
2014	Long	Mary Soon Lee	"Interregnum"
	Short	Amal El-Mohtar	"Turning the Leaves"
2015	Long	F. J. Bergmann	"100 Reasons to Have Sex with an Alien"
	Short	Marge Simon	"Shutdown"

For a complete list of past Rhysling winners, runners-up, and nominees, see the SFPA Rhysling archive at **sfpoetry.com/ra/rhysarchive.html**

SFPA Grand Master Award Winners

1999	Bruce Boston
2005	Robert Frazier
2008	Ray Bradbury
2010	Jane Yolen
2015	Marge Simon & Steve Sneyd

A SFPA Grand Master designation may be conferred by the SFPA President with consensus of the membership to an individual living at the time of selection whose body of work shall reflect the highest artistic goals of the SFPA, who shall have been actively publishing within speculative poetry for a period of no fewer than 20 years, and whose poetry has been noted to be exceptional in merit, scope, vision and innovation.

For further information, see **sfpoetry.com/grandmasters.html**

How to Join SFPA

SFPA members receive *Star∗Line*, the quarterly journal, filled with poetry, reviews, articles, and more; the annual *Rhysling Anthology*, containing the best SF/F/H poetry of the previous year (selected by the membership); and *Dwarf Stars*, an edited anthology of the best short-short speculative poetry of the previous year. Each member may nominate one short poem and one long poem for the *Rhysling Anthology* and then vote for the Rhysling Awards from the anthology. Members may nominate poems of ten lines or fewer to the *Dwarf Stars* editor and vote for that award as well. SFPA also sponsors the Elgin Awards for speculative poetry chapbooks and full-length books, and an annual poetry contest.

SFPA Membership—One Year

$40.00 • United States print:
  (*Star∗Line, Dwarf Stars,*
  Rhysling Anthology)
$50.00 • Canada
$60.00 • Mexico
$65.00 • Overseas

$30 • U.S. with *Star∗Line* as .pdf,
Dwarf Stars & *Rhysling* as print
$35 • Canada
$40 • Mexico
$45 • Overseas

$15 • .pdf only

Five Years

$180 • United States print:
  (*Star∗Line, Dwarf Stars,*
  Rhysling Anthology)
$225 • Canada
$270 • Mexico
$295 • Overseas

$135 • U.S. with Star*Line as .pdf,
rest print
$160 • Canada
$180 • Mexico
$205 • Overseas

$65 • .pdf only

Lifetime

Payable in 3 payments over 3 years.
$600 • U.S. print:
  (*Star∗Line, Dwarf Stars,*
  Rhysling Anthology)
$750 • Canada
$900 • Mexico
$975 • International

$450 • U.S. with Star*Line as .pdf,
rest print
$525 • Canada
$600 • Mexico
$675 • International

$225 • .pdf only

Failure to make all payments reverts to number of years actually paid.
All prices are in U.S. funds. Checks and money orders should be made out to the Science Fiction Poetry Association and sent to:

SFPA Treasurer
P.O. Box 907
Winchester, CA 92596

or pay online via PayPal to SFPAtreasurer@gmail.com.